for 3 - 9s

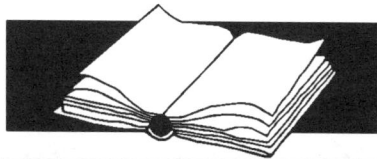

Book 12

CHRISTIAN FOCUS PUBLICATIONS

We believe that the Bible is God's word to mankind, and that it contains everything we need to know in order to be reconciled with God and to live in a way that is pleasing to him. Therefore, we believe it is vital to teach children accurately from the Bible, being careful to teach each passage's true meaning in an appropriate way, rather than selecting a 'children's message' from a Biblical passage.

© TnT Ministries
29 Buxton Gardens, Acton, London, W3 9LE
Tel: +44 (0)20 8992 0450

Published in 1999, Reprinted 2002
by Christian Focus Publications Ltd.
Geanies House, Fearn, Tain, Ross-shire, IV20 1TW
Tel: (01862) 871 011 Fax: (01862) 871 028

Cover design by Douglas McConnach

Production by Shadbolt Associates. Tel +44 (0) 20 8325 3131

This book and others in the series can be purchased from your local
Christian bookshop. Alternatively you can contact TnT Ministries direct
or place your order with the publisher.

ISBN 1-85792-407-X

TnT Ministries (which stands for Teaching and Training) was launched in February 1993 by Christians from a broad variety of denominational backgrounds who were concerned that teaching the Bible to children should be taken seriously. They have been in charge of the Sunday School of 50 teachers at St Helen's Bishopsgate, an evangelical church in the City of London, since 1984, during which time a range of Biblical teaching materials has been developed. On request, TnT Ministries also runs training days for Sunday School teachers.

CONTENTS

On the Way for 3-9s / Book 12

WEEK	SUBJECT	PAGE
	HEAVENLY MESSENGERS - overview	5
1	Nativity Play	6
2	Reassured by an Angel	10
3	Good News Proclaimed by Angels	15
4	Guided by a Star	22
5	Warned by an Angel	27
	JESUS HELPS - overview	32
6	Jesus Helps at a Wedding	33
7	Jesus Helps a Sick Son	43
8	Jesus Helps a Crippled Woman	51
9	Jesus Helps Ten Lepers	56
10	Jesus Helps a Blind Man	62
	PARABLES OF THE KINGDOM - overview	68
11	The Parable of the Sower	70
12	The Parable of the Weeds	80
13	The Parable of the Hidden Treasure and the Pearl	87
14	The Parable of the Great Feast	95

Preparation of Bible material:
Thalia Blundell
David & Christine James

Editing:
David Jackman

Illustrations:
Ben Desmond

Other Contributors:
Naomi Beak
Thalia Blundell
Julie Farell
Annie Gemmill
Debbie Levett

On the Way works on a three year syllabus. It covers the main Bible stories from Genesis to the Acts of the Apostles. All the Bible stories are taught as truth and not myth.

Each year the birth of Jesus is taught at Christmas, and the death and resurrection of Jesus at Easter. Between Christmas and Easter the syllabus deals with aspects of Jesus' life and teaching. After Easter there is a short series on the Early Church. The rest of the year is spent looking at the Old Testament stories, covering broad sweeps of Old Testament history. In this way leaders and children gain an orderly and cohesive view of God's dealings with his people throughout the Old and New Testaments.

The lessons are grouped in series, each of which is introduced by a series overview stating the aims of the series, the lesson aim for each week and an appropriate memory verse.

Every lesson, in addition to a lesson aim, has Bible study notes to enable the teacher to understand the passage, suggestions for visual aids and an activity for the children to take home. One activity is suitable for 3-5 year olds, one for 5-7 year olds and one for 7-9s.

How to Prepare a Lesson

To prepare a Sunday School lesson properly takes at least one evening (2-3 hours). It is helpful to read the Bible passage several days before teaching it to allow time to mull over what it is saying.

When preparing a lesson the following steps should be taken -

1. PRAY!

In a busy world this is very easy to forget. We are unable to understand God's word without his help and we need to remind ourselves of that fact before we start.

2. READ THE BIBLE PASSAGE

This should be done *before* reading the lesson manual. Our resource is the Bible, not what someone says about it. The Bible study notes in the lesson manual are a commentary on the passage to help you understand it.

3. LOOK AT THE LESSON AIM

This should reflect the main teaching of the passage. Plan how that can be packaged appropriately for the age group you teach.

4. STORYTELLING

Decide how to tell the Bible story. Is it appropriate to recapitulate on what has happened in previous weeks? Will you involve the children in the presentation of the story? What sort of questions are appropriate to use? How will you ascertain what has been understood? Is there anything in the story that should be applied to their lives?

5. VISUAL AIDS

What type of visual aid will help bring the story alive for the children? Simple pictures may be appropriate. For stories with a lot of movement it may be better to use flannelgraphs or suedegraphs. In some instances models may be appropriate, e.g. the paralysed man being let down through a hole in the roof. Do remember that visual aids take time to make and this will need to be built into your lesson preparation.

6. CRAFT ACTIVITIES

Many of the craft activities require prior preparation by the teacher so do not leave it until the night before!

Benefits of On the Way

- Encourages the leaders to study the Bible for themselves.
- Chronological approach gives leaders and children a sequential view of God's dealings with his people.
- Each lesson has 3 age related craft activities.
- Everything you need is in the one book, so there is no need to buy children's activity books.
- Undated materials allow you to use the lessons to fit your situation without wastage.
- Once you have the entire syllabus, there is no need to repurchase.

Teacher's Challenge

Located throughout this book are cartoons highlighting some aspects of the Bible passages. Hidden in one or more of these cartoons is a bookworm (see box on right - not actual size).

If you consider yourself observant and want a challenge, count the number of times the bookworm appears in this edition. The correct answer is on the back page. Don't look until you are sure you have found them all!

Heavenly Messengers

Overview

Week 1   NATIVITY PLAY

Week 2   REASSURED BY AN ANGEL   *Matthew 1:18-25*
To show how God confirms that Jesus is the promised Saviour.

Week 3   GOOD NEWS PROCLAIMED BY ANGELS   *Luke 2:1-20*
To teach that Jesus is the Saviour of the world.

Week 4   GUIDED BY A STAR   *Matthew 2:1-12*
To teach that Jesus is King and is to be worshipped.

Week 5   WARNED BY AN ANGEL   *Matthew 2:13-23*
To teach that God's plan cannot be thwarted.

Series Aims

1.   To understand the stories in their context.
2.   To understand that this baby was God, the Saviour of the world.

Although the Christmas story is a familiar one, the younger children will not have remembered all the details from last year. Also, they may have absorbed the mixture of fantasy and fact that is often presented in their school and on the television. We need to tell these stories in such a way that the children are filled with awe and wonder that God became man for our sake - that this helpless little baby came as the Saviour of the world (John 4:42).

Try to convey the excitement of the occasion, as well as God's control over events - sending the angel to reassure Joseph as to the identity of the coming child; the census occurring so that the baby was born at Bethlehem (Micah 5:2); bringing the poor and the rich, Jews and Gentiles, to worship him; warning Joseph so that the family could escape to Egypt (week 5). For the older children, show how Jesus' birth fulfilled the prophecies about the coming Messiah.

The Nativity play (week 1) can be slotted in at a convenient point in the programme or can be discarded if wished.

Memory Work

3-5s   Jesus is the Saviour of the world

John 4:42

5-9s   We know that Jesus really is the Saviour of the world.

John 4:42

Cast

Narrator
Mary
Joseph
People of Nazareth, people of Bethlehem
Angel Gabriel
Innkeeper
Chief Angel + angels
Shepherds 1, 2 and 3 + shepherds
3 Wise men + Pages
Herod

Stage Set

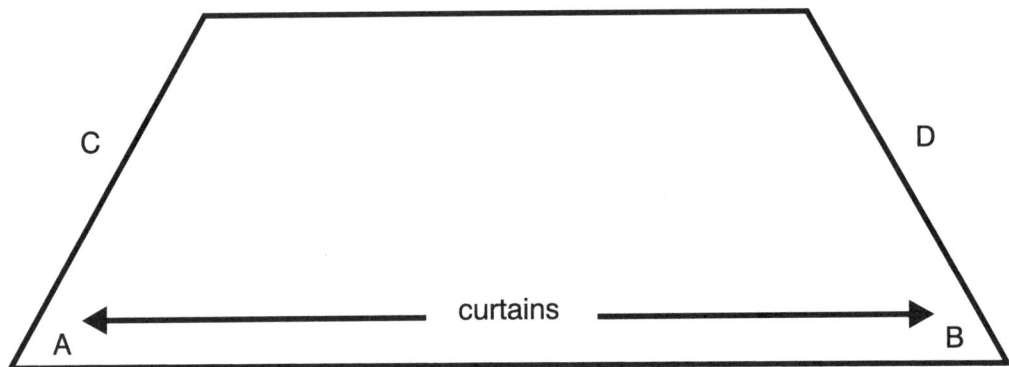

If possible, a moving star should run between B and centre stage, otherwise position the star over centre stage.

Play

Narrator enters and stands at A.

Narrator   Nearly 2,000 years ago Mary and Joseph lived in the busy town of Nazareth.

Curtains open to reveal the people of Nazareth going about their business. Some are sitting and selling their wares, others are buying or passing through with pots on their heads, etc. Mary and Joseph walk across the stage. The curtains close.

Narrator   Mary had promised to marry Joseph. One day Mary had a very special visitor.

Curtains open to show Mary alone at centre stage. Angel Gabriel enters from D.

Narrator   It was the Angel Gabriel with a message for Mary from God.

Mary looks frightened.

Gabriel Don't be afraid, Mary. God has been kind to you. You are going to have a special baby. You must call him Jesus. He will be great and will be called the Son of God. He will be a great King and his kingdom will never end.

Mary How can this be possible? I don't have a husband.

Gabriel God's Holy Spirit will come upon you. For this reason the holy baby will be the Son of God.

Mary I am the Lord's servant. Let everything happen to me just as you have said.

Mary exits towards C and Gabriel towards D. Joseph enters and lies down.

Narrator When Joseph heard that Mary was going to have a baby he was very unhappy and thought that they should not get married. So, one night, God sent an angel to him in a dream.

Enter chief angel.

Angel Joseph, don't be afraid to marry Mary. The baby is from God not man. When he is born you must name him 'Jesus', because he will save his people from their sins.

Curtains close.

Narrator Joseph did as the angel said and married Mary (pause).
When the time came for the baby to be born the Roman Emperor ordered a list of all the people to be made. This meant that everyone had to go to the town where their family came from. Joseph and Mary went to Bethlehem, the town of King David, because they were his descendants. So, the Old Testament prophecy of the Messiah being born in Bethlehem came true.
Mary's baby was ready to be born, but Bethlehem was full of people coming to be listed.

Curtains open to show the people arriving in Bethlehem. They are carrying bags and gradually exit at different 'house doorways'. There is a notice saying, 'Inn' attached at the back of the stage. As the last people are leaving the stage Joseph and Mary enter and move towards the Inn. Joseph knocks on the Inn door. The Innkeeper appears.

Joseph Please, sir, do you have any room in your inn?

Innkeeper Sorry, there is no room left.

Joseph My wife's baby is ready to be born and we have nowhere to stay.

Innkeeper The only place I have free is the stable where the animals are. You could stay there.

Joseph   Thank you, that will be fine.

Innkeeper   Follow me, please.

Mary and Joseph follow the Innkeeper through the Inn door.   Curtains close. Background music 'While shepherds watched'.

Narrator   That same night some shepherds were looking after their sheep in the nearby hills.

Curtains open to show the shepherds sitting down at the D side of centre stage.

Narrator   Suddenly an angel appeared.

The chief angel leads the angels onto the stage from side C.   The shepherds look frightened.

Angel   Don't be afraid! I come with good news for you which will bring joy to all people. This very day, in Bethlehem, your Saviour has been born. He is Christ, the Lord. You will find him wrapped in strips of cloth and lying in a manger.

All Angels   Glory to God in the highest heaven and peace to his people on earth.

Shepherd 1   Let's go to Bethlehem and find this baby.

Angels exit at C, while shepherds get up, pick up their sheep and exit at D.   Curtains close with 'Inn' notice pinned to one of them where they join.   Shepherds enter at B and move to the Inn door.   As they get there the curtains open to show Mary, Joseph and the baby lying in the manger. Background music 'Hark! The herald angels sing'.

Shepherd 2   The angels visited us in the fields and told us that your baby is the promised Saviour, Christ the Lord.

Shepherd 3   This is a wonderful day.

Shepherd 1   We can have peace with God.

All the shepherds kneel down to worship the baby. Curtains close. Background music 'We three kings'.

Narrator   There were some other visitors.   Some Wise Men saw a special star and followed it, knowing it would lead them to a new-born king.   They came first to the palace of King Herod.

Wise Men and Pages enter at B. Herod appears from behind the curtains at centre stage and walks across to the Wise Men.

Wise Man 1   Where is the baby born to be King of the Jews?

Wise Man 2   We have followed his star all the way from our homes (points at star).

Herod   The Scriptures tell us that he will be born in Bethlehem. Go and make a careful search for him. When you have found him come back and tell me so that I, too, may worship him.

Herod exits where he entered.

Narrator   Herod was very jealous when he heard about a new king. He wanted to know where the baby was in order to kill him.

Star moves to centre stage, followed by wise men and pages. Children sing, 'Follow the star' verses 1 and 2.

Narrator   They followed the star to Bethlehem. It stopped above the place where the baby was.

Curtains open to show Mary, Joseph and the baby. Wise Men and Pages enter the stable, kneel down and place their gifts before the baby. Children sing, 'Follow the star' verse 3. The rest of the cast enter and group around the central characters.

Narrator   Let us pray. Dear Lord Jesus, thank you for coming to earth as a baby to bring us salvation. Thank you for the Bible, which tells us the truth about you. Help us to worship you this Christmas as our King and Saviour.

Children sing, 'Away in a Manger'. Curtains close

Carols	
While shepherds watched	(Junior Praise 285)
Hark! the herald angels sing	(Junior Praise 69)
We three kings of Orient are	(Junior Praise 271)
Follow the star	(Chappell of Bond St, 50 New Bond St, London W1Y 9HA)
Away in a manger	(Junior Praise 12)

Props
Mats, baskets, etc. for the people of Nazareth
Duster for Mary
Bags for the people of Bethlehem
'Inn' notice
Baby wrapped in a shawl in a box of straw
Sheep
Star
Gold, frankincense & myrrh

Preparation:
Read Matthew 1:18-25 using the Bible study notes to help you.

Lesson Aim:
To show how God confirms that Jesus is the promised Saviour.

1:25   This makes it clear that Jesus' conception was due to activity of God and not man. The implication is that Joseph and Mary had a normal marriage relationship after the birth of Jesus (Matthew 13:55-56).

1:18   Betrothal/engagement was a binding agreement and could only be broken by divorce. Unfaithfulness during the period of betrothal was regarded as adultery.

1:19   There were 2 recognised ways of divorce - a) court action with its attendant publicity, b) giving a writ in the presence of 2 witnesses. Joseph chose the latter, tempering justice with mercy.

1:20   The angel of the Lord was a heavenly being sent by God to men as his personal spokesman/messenger, to give guidance and offer instructions. Do ensure that the children realise the high position of the angel and the importance of his message - the picture in their minds will be of girls dressed in long white dresses with gold wings and tinsel crowns!

1:21   Jesus is the Greek form of the Hebrew Joshua - 'The Lord saves'.

1:22-23   See Isaiah 7:14.

Lesson Plan

This is the first taught lesson of the series about heavenly messengers. Start by sending a message down the line of children using Chinese whispers. Was that a good way to send a message? How else could they send a message to someone? They could write a letter, make a telephone call, send smoke signals, use Morse code, send a messenger. Pin up pictures to illustrate the different ways. Talk about the importance of sending a message that can be understood. In today's true story from the Bible we will find out about a man who did not know what to do for the best. Ask the children to listen carefully so that they can tell you the man's name, his problem and how God sent him a message.

At the end of the story go over the answers to the questions and teach the memory verse.

Visual Aids

Pictures to illustrate ways of sending messages.

A home made advent calendar can be used for the series. The backing card/paper will need to be A1 size. Use 16 pictures - 4 for each week (see diagram). The covering of each picture is better removed completely, rather than folded back. The pictures can be different sizes.

Pictures for advent calendar:

1. Mary
2. Joseph
3. Angel
4. Open book - God with us (to bring out the prophecy)
5. Mary and Joseph on their way to Bethlehem
6. No room at the Inn
7. Baby in the manger
8. Shepherds in the field
9. Wise men and a star
10. Herod
11. Bethlehem
12. Gifts
13. Angel
14. Family escaping to Egypt
15. Mother crying
16. Return to Nazareth (small child rather than a baby)

Heavenly Messengers

1	2	3	4
5	6	7	
8	9	10	
11	12	13	
14	15	16	

Activities / 3 - 5s

Make a Christmas card. Photocopy page 11 on paper and page 12 on coloured card for each child. Prior to the lesson fold page 12 in half with the Bible verse over the top of the doors on the front and the words on the back. Cut around the doors and fold them back along the dotted lines. Cut out the figures from page 11 and place in an envelope for each child. The children colour the figures and glue them onto the card. Mary, Joseph and the baby are placed inside the card and the star is glued above the doors on the outside. Write the child's name after 'from' on the back of the card.

Activities / 5 - 7s

Photocopy pages 13 and 14 for each child. Prior to the lesson cut out the wheel from page 13 and the hatched areas from page 14. The children colour the picture and the figures on the wheel. Attach the wheel behind the picture using a split pin paper fastener at X. Turn the wheel to tell the story. The sequence is blank, angel, Mary and Joseph, blank.

Activities / 7 - 9s

Make a Christmas card. Follow the instructions for the 3-5s, but the children can cut out their own figures from page 11.

Activities / 3-5s and 7-9s

Jesus is the Saviour of the world. John 4:42

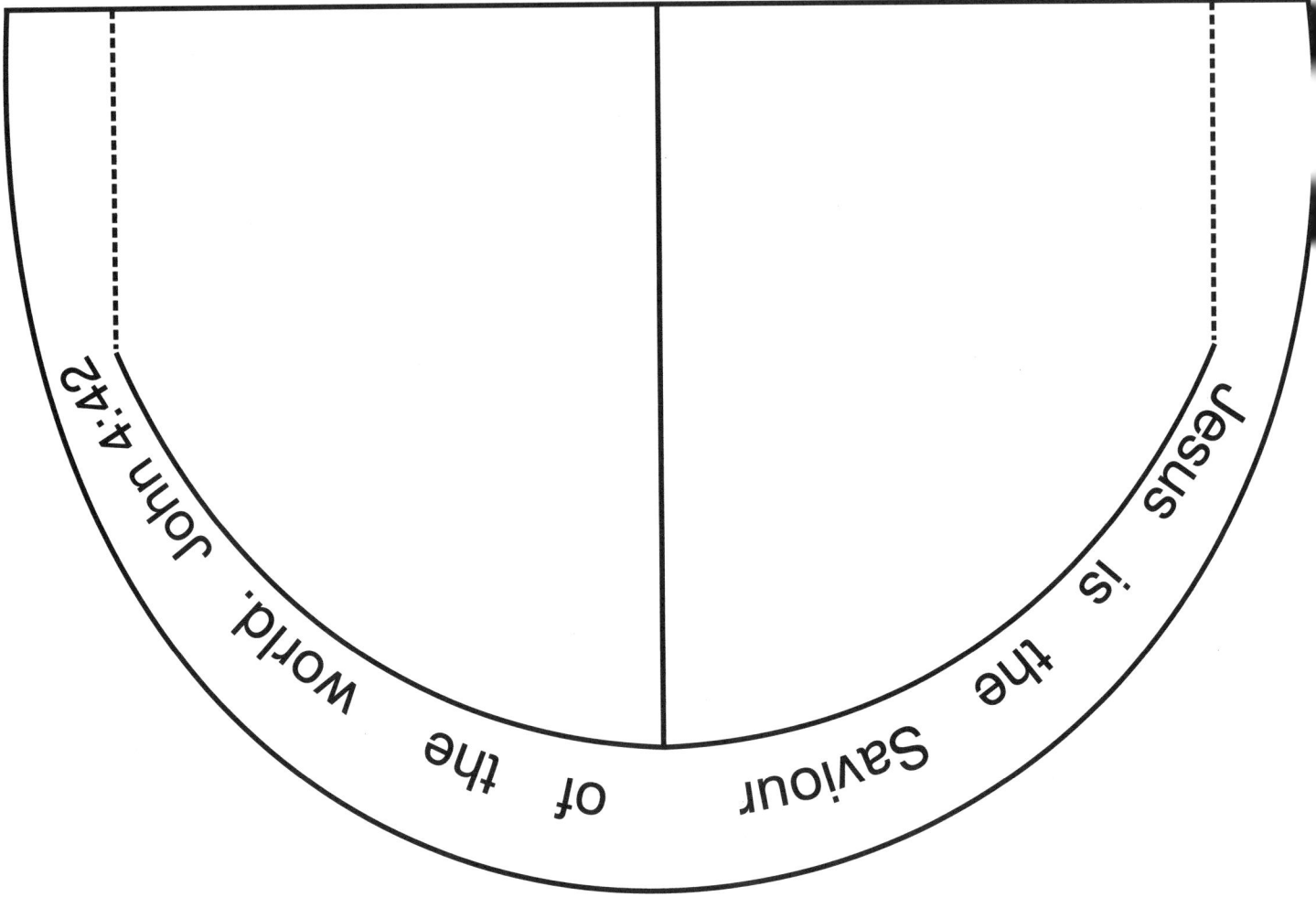

Happy Christmas
with love
from

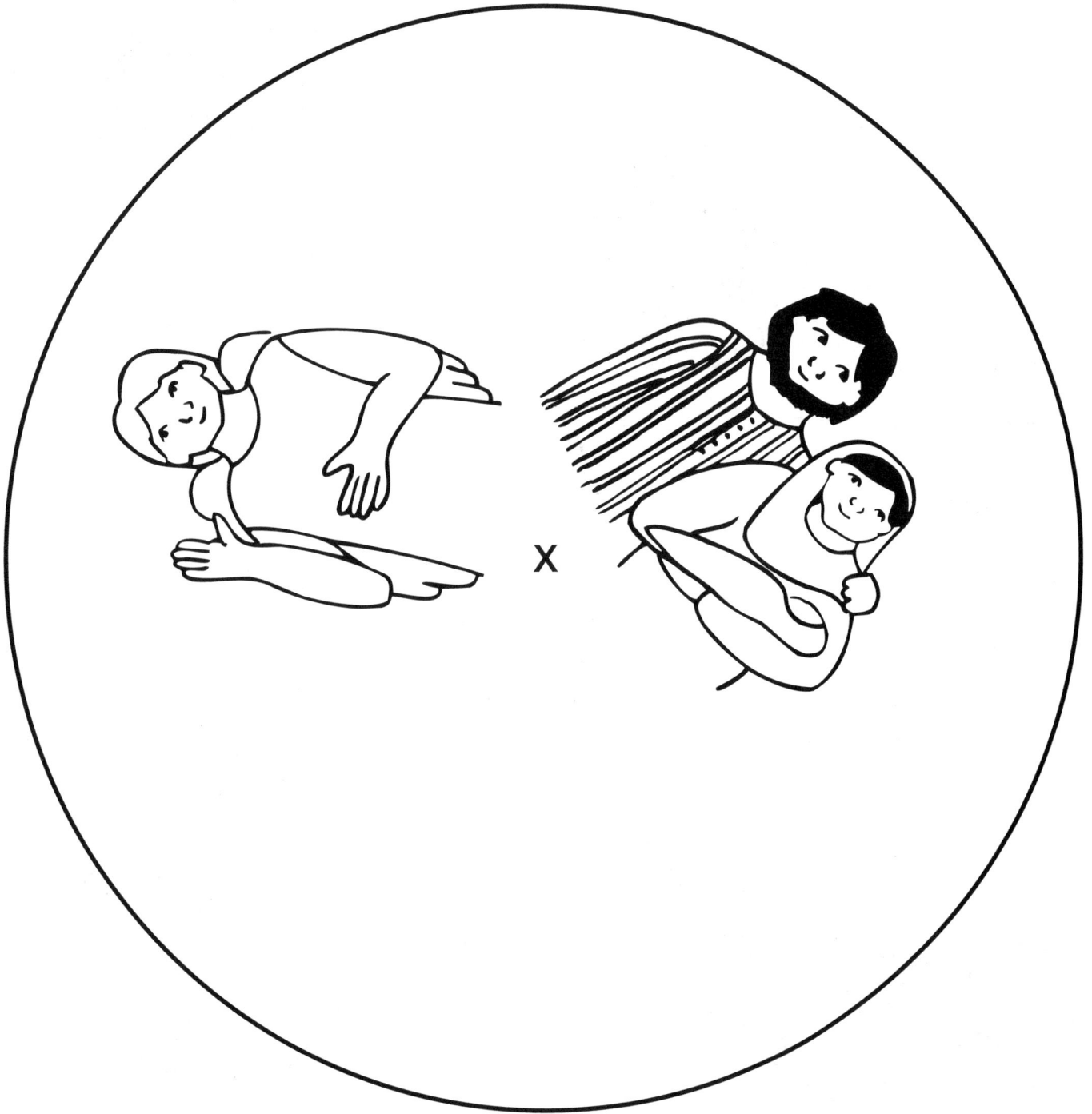

X

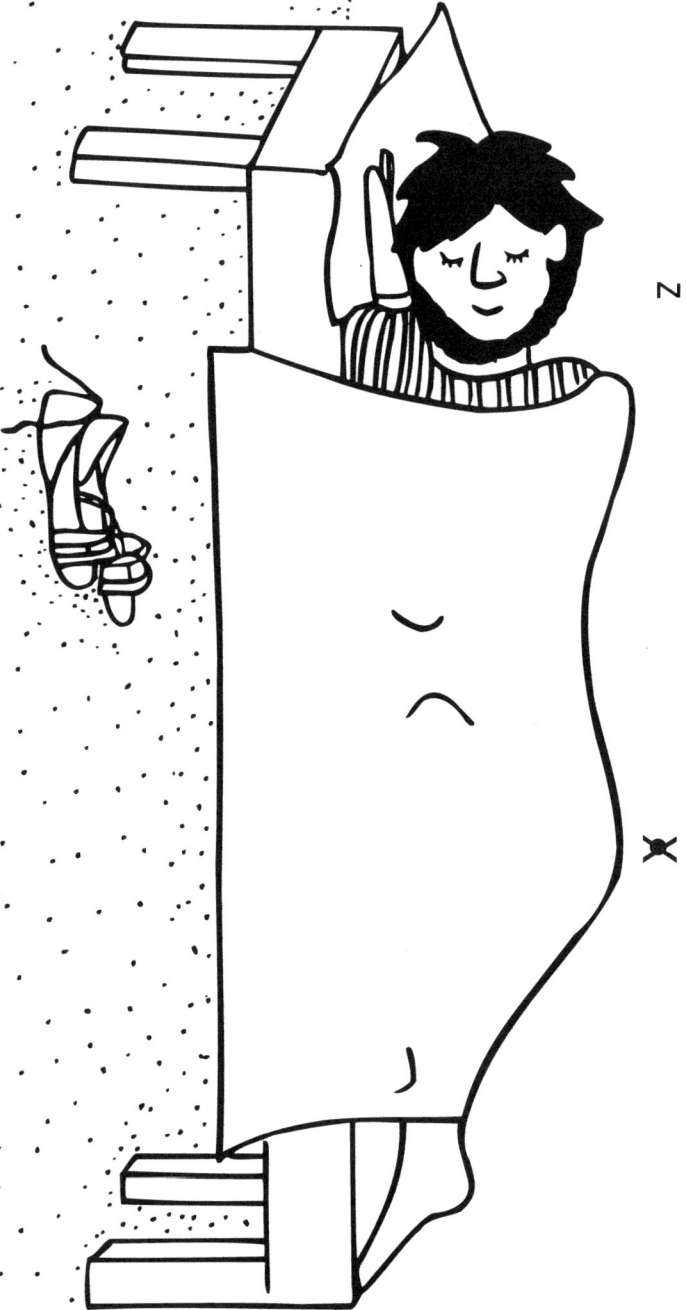

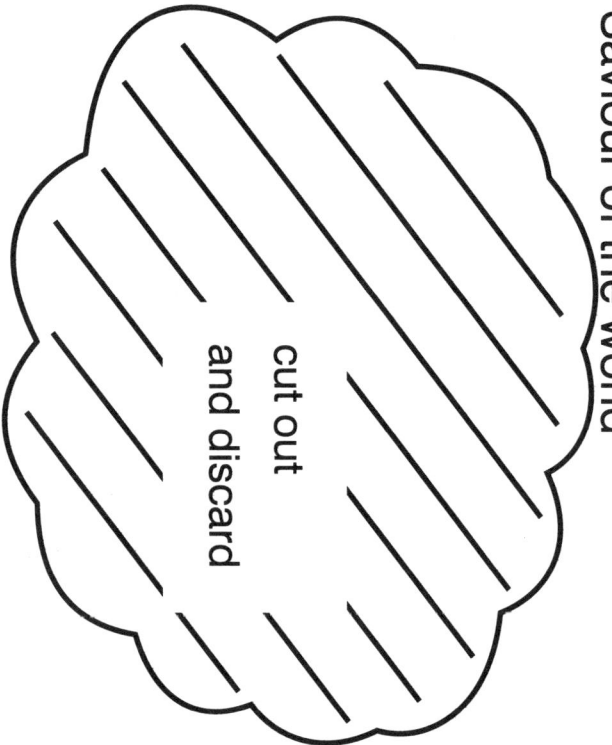

cut out
and discard

We know that Jesus really is the Saviour of the world

John 4:42

Preparation:
Read Luke 2:1-20, using the Bible study notes to help you.

2:1-3   The decree of a Roman Caesar was used by God to fulfil his purposes, revealed in the OT prophecies, that Jesus should be born in Bethlehem (Micah 5:2).

2:7   Strips of cloth were the normal way of wrapping a baby. The baby was placed diagonally on a square of cloth and 2 corners were turned over his body, one over his feet, and one under his head. The whole was then fastened by strips wound around the outside.

2:8   At this point in time shepherds were a rough group of men, often despised by more affluent and 'religious' people because their unsociable hours separated them from the worshipping community. They were not a group to whom one would expect God to reveal his Son.

2:9   Cf. the Shekinah glory (Exodus 24:16, 1 Kings 8:10-11).

Lesson Aim:
To teach that Jesus is the Saviour of the world.

2:10   The good news was for all the people, as promised years before to Abraham (Genesis 12:2-3).

2:12   The shepherds were given explicit instructions as confirmation that this baby was the Saviour.

Lesson Plan

Start by asking the children how they can attract someone's attention, e.g. calling out, waving, a bright light (lighthouse), a siren (fire engine, ambulance), a beacon. Pin up pictures to illustrate the different ways. Remind the children of last week's lesson. Joseph knew he needed someone to tell him what to do. In today's true story from the Bible we will hear about some people who did not know they needed a message. Ask the children to listen carefully so that they can tell you who the people were, how they got their message, and what message they were given.

At the end of the story go over the answers to the questions and revise the memory verse.

Visual Aids

Pictures to illustrate ways of attracting attention.
To illustrate the story see instructions for the Advent calendar on page 10 (Visual aids for week 2).

Activities / 3 - 5s

Make an angel mobile. Each child requires page 17 photocopied on card, 1 wire coat hanger, 1 tinsel garland, glitter glue (optional) and 4 different lengths of cotton thread. Prior to the lesson cut out the 4 angels from page 17. Cut along all solid lines,

discarding the hatched area. Fold the wings so that slots A and B fit into each other. Fold down the arms at the shoulders. Attach a length of cotton thread to the head. The children colour the angels and decorate with glitter glue. Wind the tinsel garland around the coat hanger. Hang the angels from the coat hanger at different heights to make a mobile.

Activities / 5 - 7s

Photocopy pages 18 and 19 for each child. Page 18 can be photocopied on coloured paper if preferred. Prior to the lesson cut along the solid lines on page 18 and fold back along the dotted lines to make windows. The children colour the pictures on page 19, then put glue around the pictures and stick it behind page 18. Make sure that the windows still open. The children number the windows from 1-5 in the order of the story. (**NB** the windows are not in the correct order on the page.)

Activities / 7 - 9s

Make a singing angel. Photocopy pages 16, 20 and 21 on card for each child. This activity takes time to make up so all the cutting out needs to be done in advance.

Activity for 7-9s

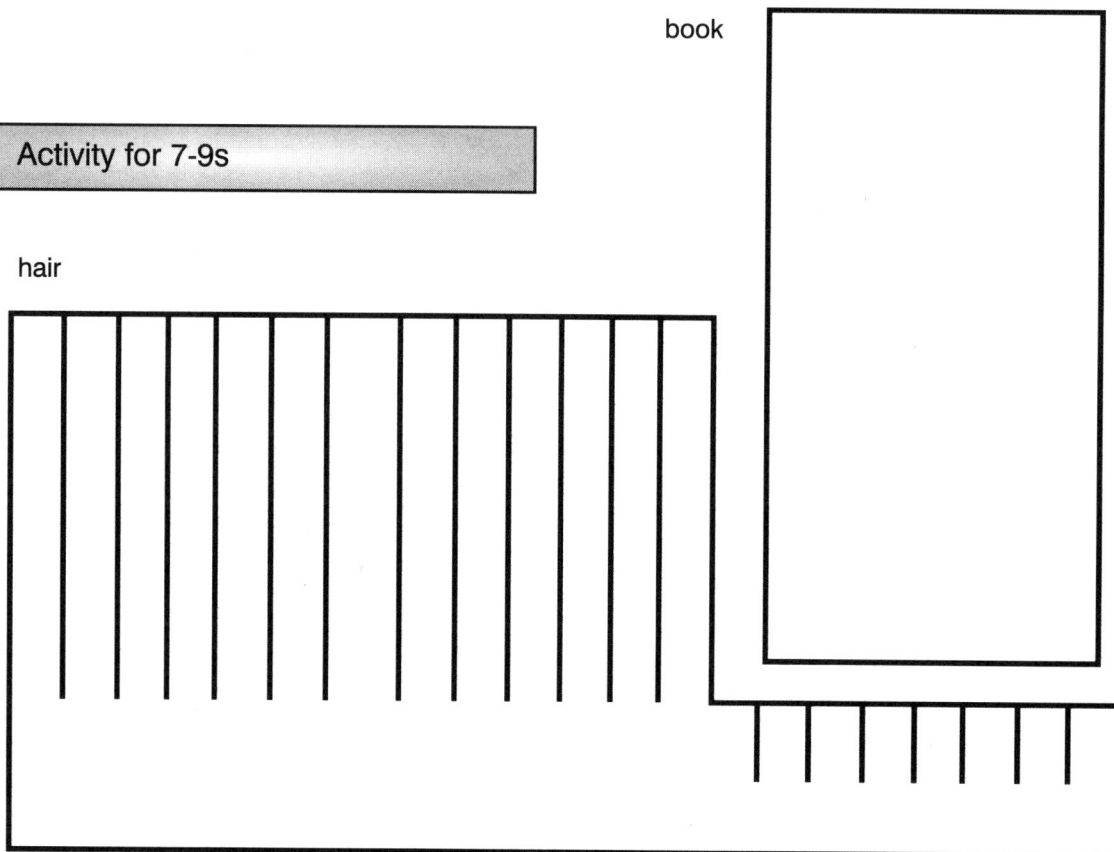

Instructions
- Roll the large square into a tube and glue. The section above the dotted line will be the head. Either draw on a face or cut out eyes, nose and mouth from coloured paper and glue in place. The mouth must be round to show the angel singing.
- Take the body and cut slits at the neck where marked. Fold back along the dotted line and glue around the tube beneath the face to make a conical body. Glue the cone together at the back or staple at the base.
- Glue the arms on either side of the body with the hands projecting forwards so that the angel can hold a book.
- Fold the small rectangle in half to form a book and glue to the insides of the hands so that the angel can 'read' it.
- Concertina fold the long strip of card at approximately 0.5 cm. Intervals. Place around the angel's neck to form a ruff and glue the ends together.
- Fold the wings along the dotted lines and glue the centre section to the back of the angel. Cut slits in the hair where indicated. Pull each strand of hair over a scissors blade to curl it. Glue the hair onto the head.
- Cut out the star and glue the tab inside the top of the head at the back. ·

Make one before the lesson to show the children.

book

hair

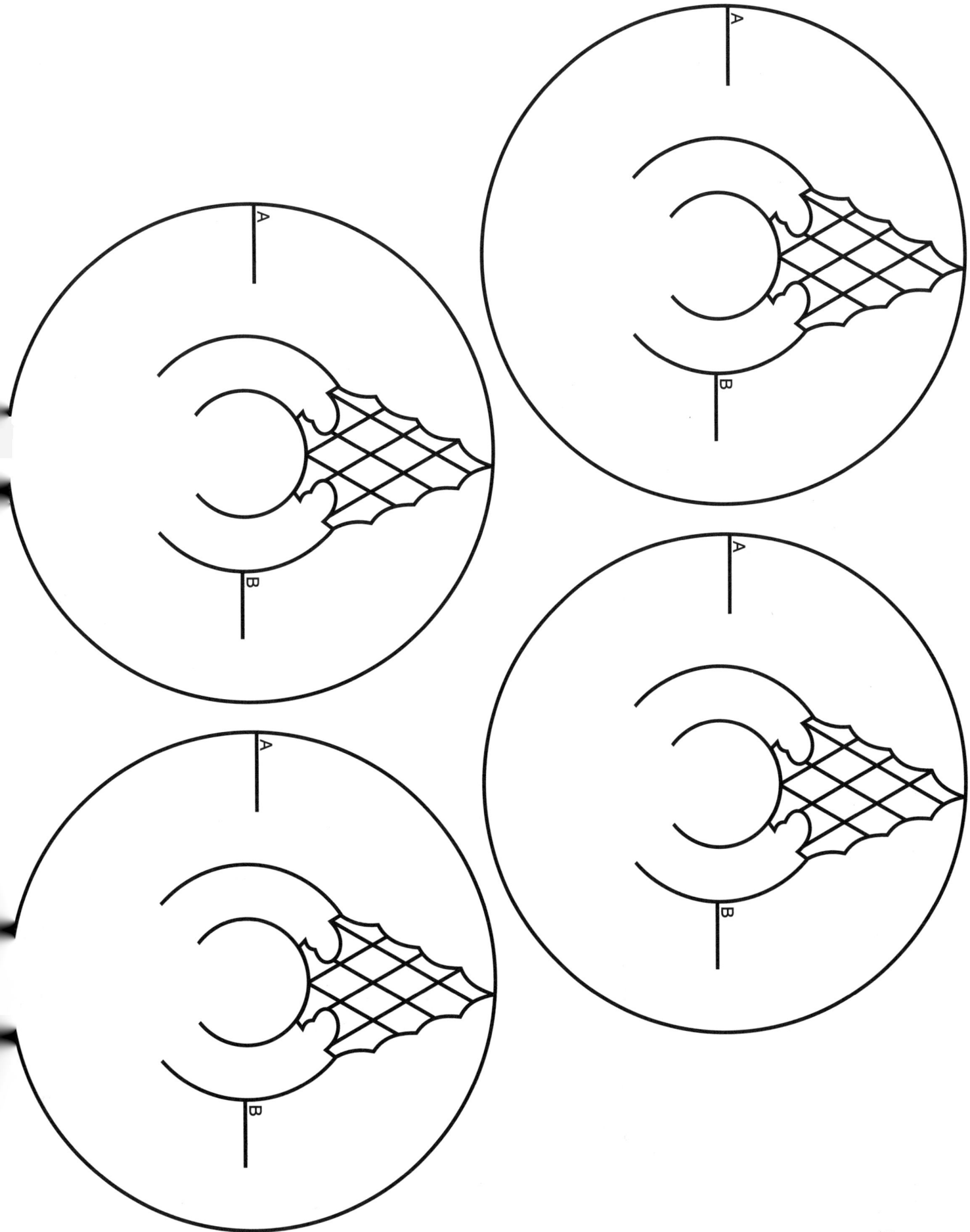

The Shepherds'
Story

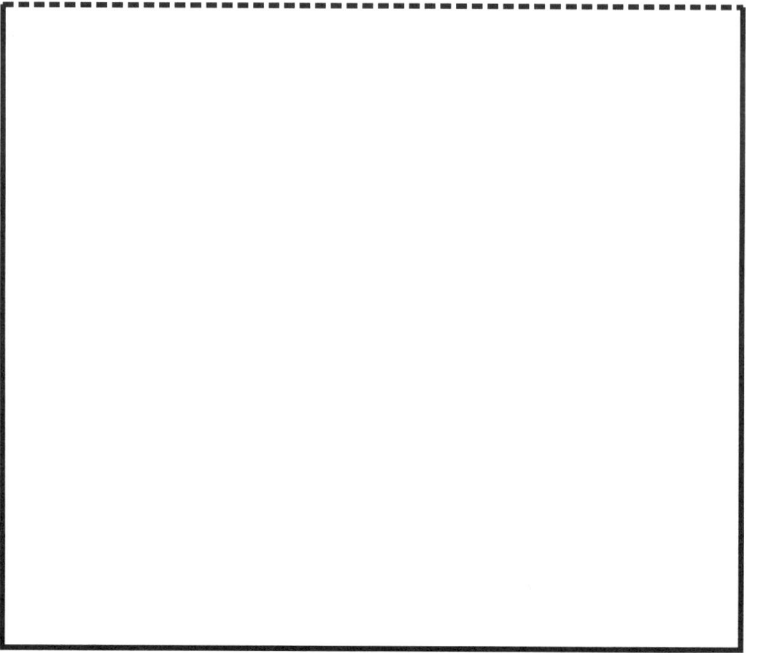

18

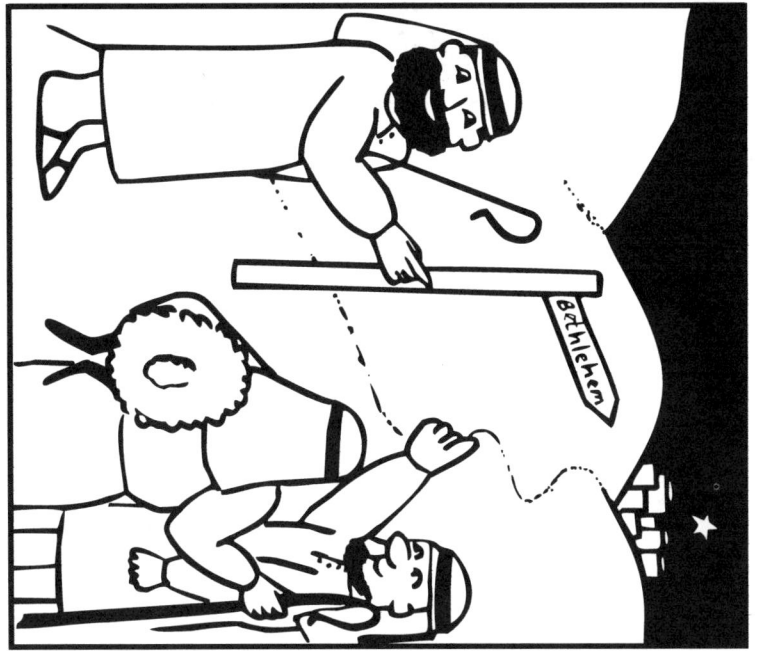

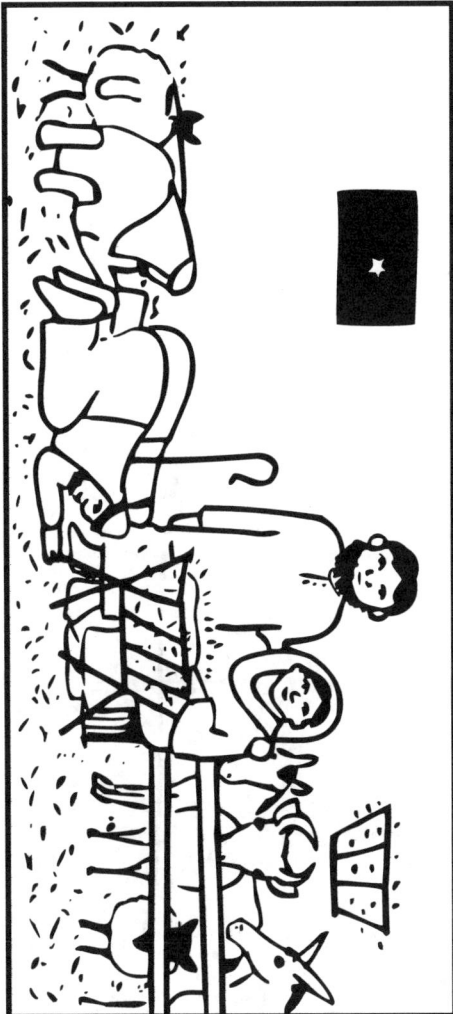

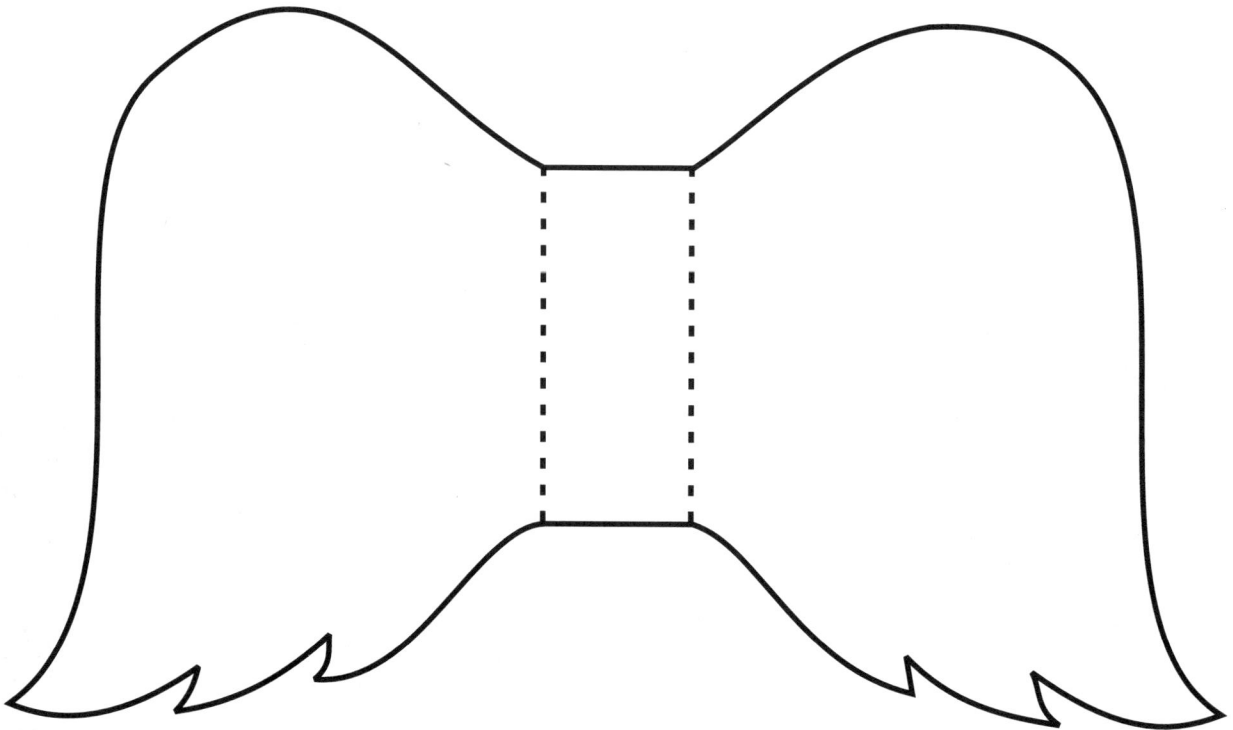

arm

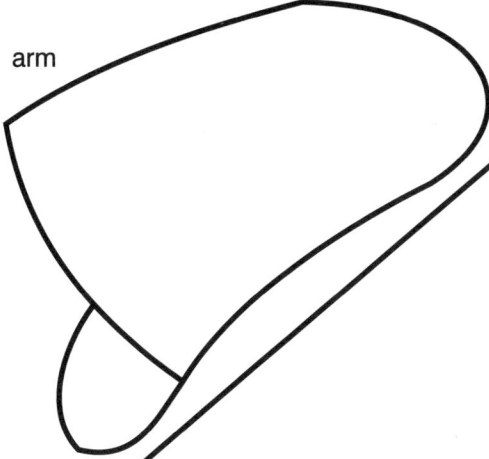

star

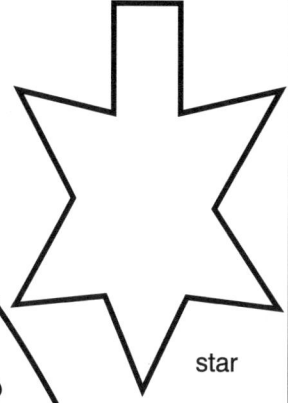

John 4:42.

We know that Jesus really is the Saviour of the world.

body

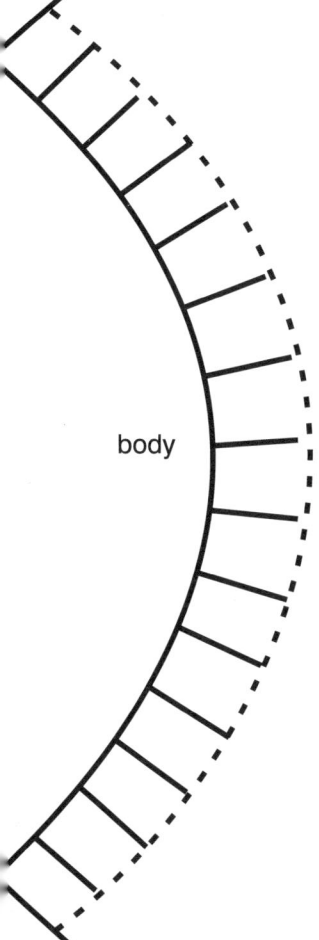

arm

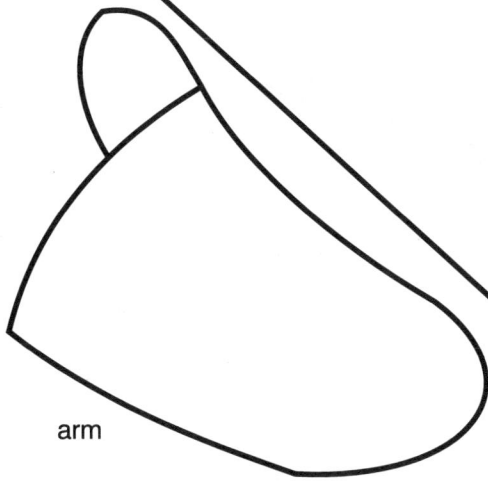

ruff

Preparation:
Read Matthew 2:1-12, using the Bible study notes to help you.

Lesson Aim:
To teach that Jesus is King and is to be worshipped.

In this story we see the Gentiles coming to worship Jesus (Isaiah 42:6, Luke 2:32).

2:1   Herod the Great (40 - 4 BC) was a puppet King under the Romans. Wise Men (Magi) were astrologers and probably came from Persia or regions round about.
Jerusalem, the capital city, was the obvious place to go for information.

2:2   It was believed that a new star signified the presence of a great man.

2:3   Herod was known to be a cruel man, so if he was upset it was no wonder that the rest of Jerusalem was also upset!

2:4   Herod's question demonstrates that he had no doubt that it was to the Messiah the Wise Men were referring.

2:5-6   Micah 5:2.

2:7-8   Herod is already plotting how to get rid of the Messiah.

2:10   Cf. Numbers 24:17 - the Jews interpreted this verse as referring to the Messiah.

2:11   This event took place some time between Jesus being 40 days old (Luke 2:22-24) and 2 years (Matthew 2:16), and common sense tells us that the family would not be still living in the stable. The 3 gifts is the reason why the wise men are portrayed as numbering 3 - although there is no definite evidence for this.

Psalm 72:10 and Isaiah 49:7 explain why the Magi came to be thought of as Kings. The gifts were given as a mark of homage to a king. Gold signified kingship, frankincense - divinity, and myrrh for a man who would die (myrrh was used in embalming bodies).

Lesson Plan

Talk to the children about going on a journey, e.g. to see Granny. How do you know where to go? What sort of things could help you find your way, e.g. a map, a compass, a guide? In today's true story from the Bible we will learn about some people who knew they must go on a journey, but did not know where to go. Ask the children to listen carefully so that they can tell you who the people were, why they were making their journey and how they knew where to go. Recap on the previous 2 weeks using a question and answer format.

At the end of the story go over the answer to the questions and revise the memory verse.

Visual Aids

A map, a compass and a picture of someone who knows where to go, e.g. the pilot of a plane. Use the advent calendar to illustrate the story - see visual aids for week 2 on page 10.

Activities / 3 - 5s

Make a star calendar. Each child requires page 24 photocopied on card, a length of ribbon to make a hanging loop and a calendar for the following year (available from stationers). Prior to the lesson cut out the star and punch a hole at X. The children decorate their stars with gummed paper shapes. Staple the calendar to the bottom point of the star and thread the ribbon through the hole at the top, tying it to make a hanging loop. If calendars are unobtainable photocopy page 24 on card twice for each child and provide 2 lengths of ribbon. Cut out both stars. Cut one star from the top point to the centre (see diagram) and the other star from the bottom point to the centre. Punch a hole in each half of the top and bottom points of each star. The children decorate both stars. Slot the stars together at right angles to make a 3D star. Thread one length of ribbon through the 4 holes at the top of the star and knot to make a hanging loop. Thread the second length of ribbon through the 4 holes at the bottom of the star, knot and use to suspend a rectangle of card with the memory verse written on it.

Activities / 5 - 7s

Make a Wise Men mobile. Each child requires page 25 photocopied on card, a wire coat hanger and 1 tinsel garland. Prior to the lesson cut out the Wise Men, arms and star and place in an envelope for each child. Attach a length of cotton thread to the head of each Wise Man and to the point of the star. The children colour the star gold or silver and colour the Wise Men and their arms. Make each man by gluing the sides together to form a cone. Glue one end of the arms over the hatched area to make a circle. Slip the arms over the man's head and staple to the body at the back (see diagram). Wind the tinsel garland around the coat hanger, then attach the 3 men and the star (see diagram).

Activities / 7 - 9s

To make an origami star photocopy page 26 on yellow paper for each child.

Instructions
- Cut out both squares.
- Take one square and fold in half corner to corner to make a triangle. Press along the crease.
- Open out and repeat with the other 2 corners.
- Open out and fold in half side to side to make a rectangle. Press along the crease.
- Open out and repeat with the other 2 sides.
- Cut along the crease line in the centre of the side half way to the centre point (f-g) - see diagram.
- Repeat with the other 3 sides.
- Fold side f-b to crease b-x and press fold. Repeat with side h-b.
- Repeat with the other 3 corners.
- Glue h-b over f-b and hold firmly for a count of 20 so that it sticks.
- Repeat with the other 3 corners.
- The star should now look like this (see diagram). (Dotted lines indicate underneath folds.)
- Make up the second square in the same way.
- Using sellotape, stick the stars back to back either as a 4 or an 8 pointed star.
- Using a needle and cotton, put a hanging loop at the top point of the star.

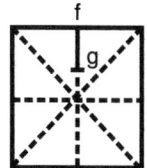

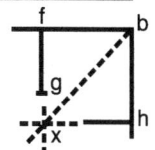

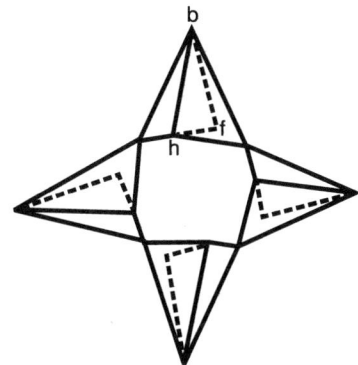

Stars can be made using 2 squares of gummed yellow paper instead of a photocopied sheet.

N. B. When doing any kind of paper folding exercise make sure that all the children have completed the fold before going on to the next one.

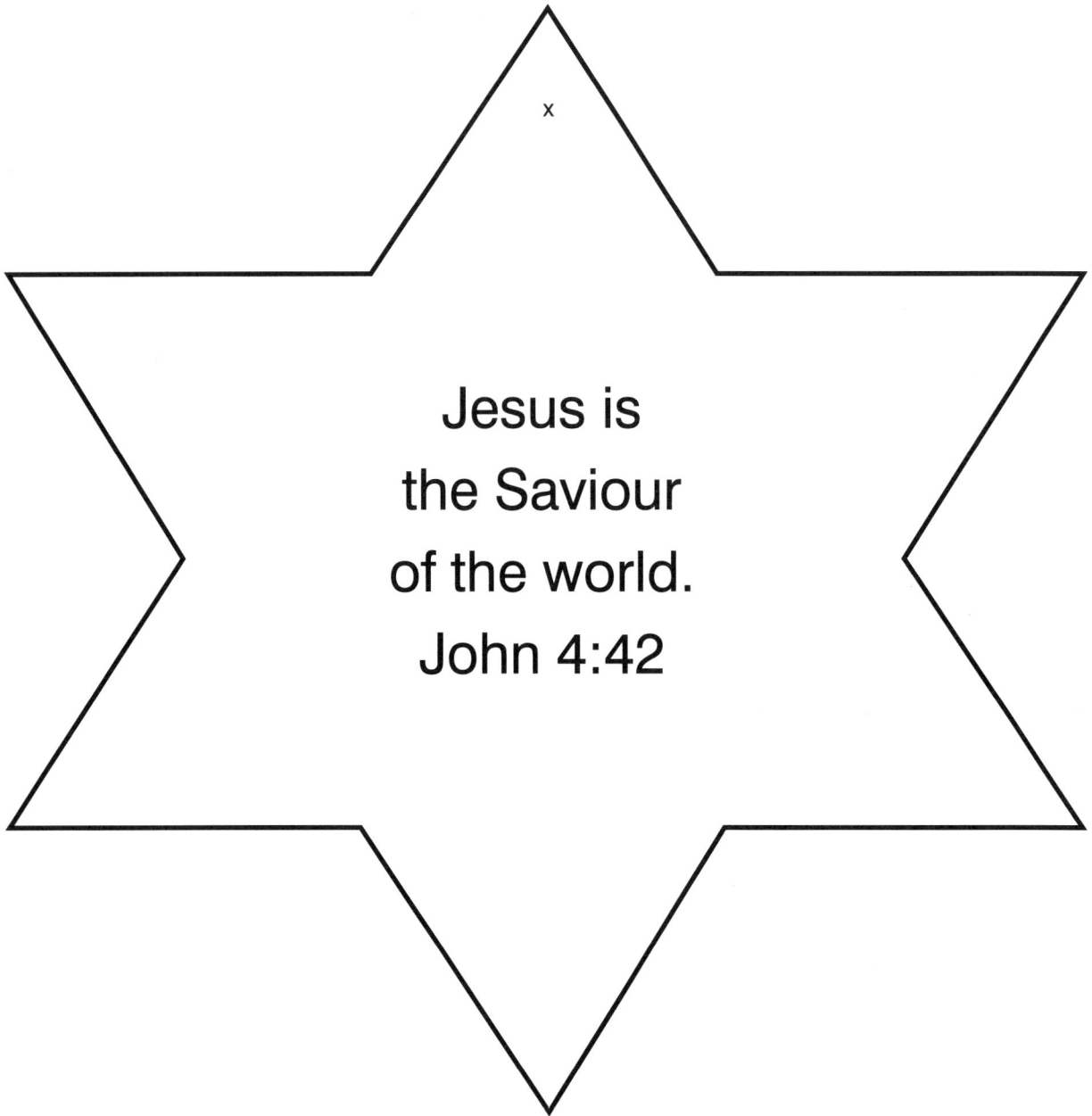

Jesus is
the Saviour
of the world.
John 4:42

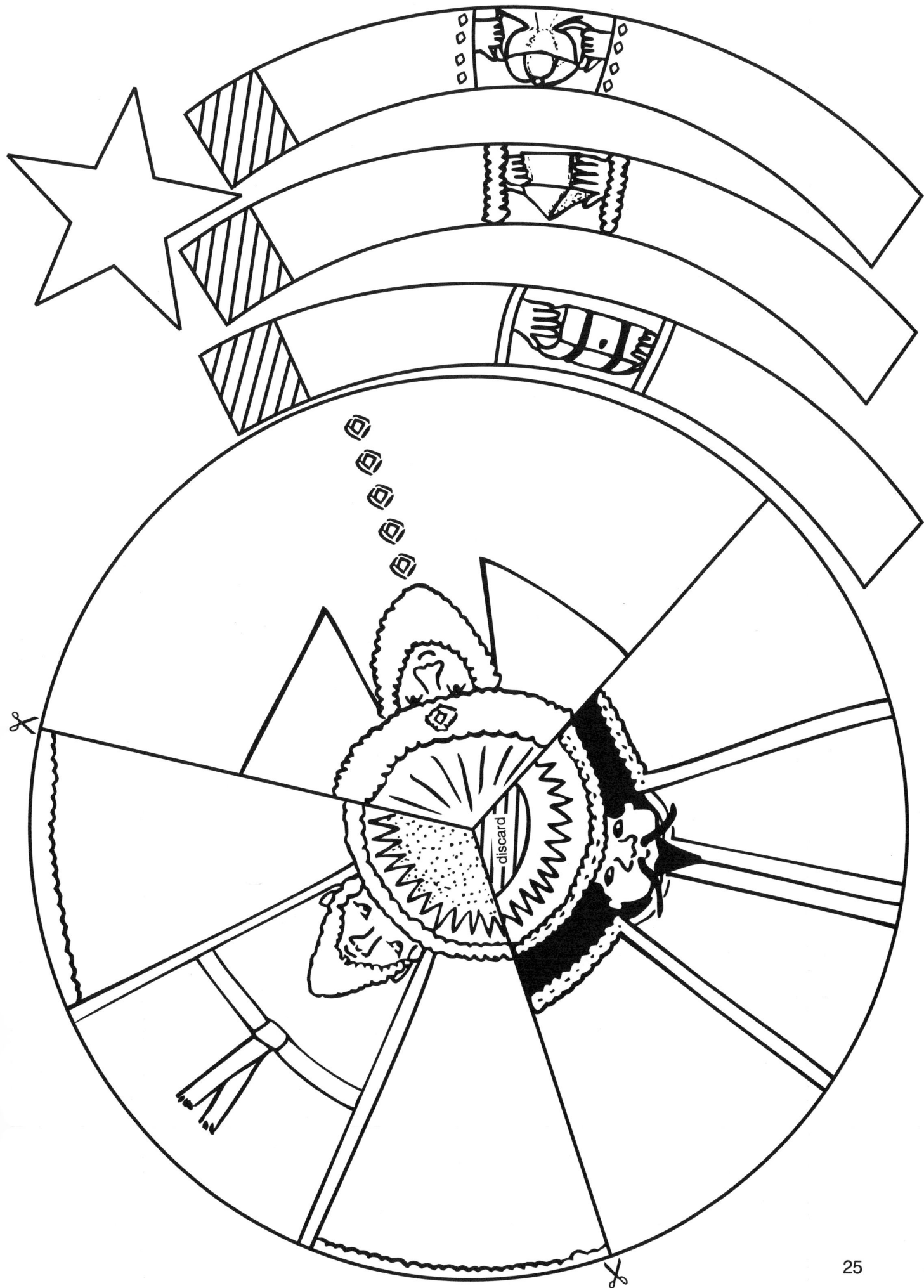

discard

25

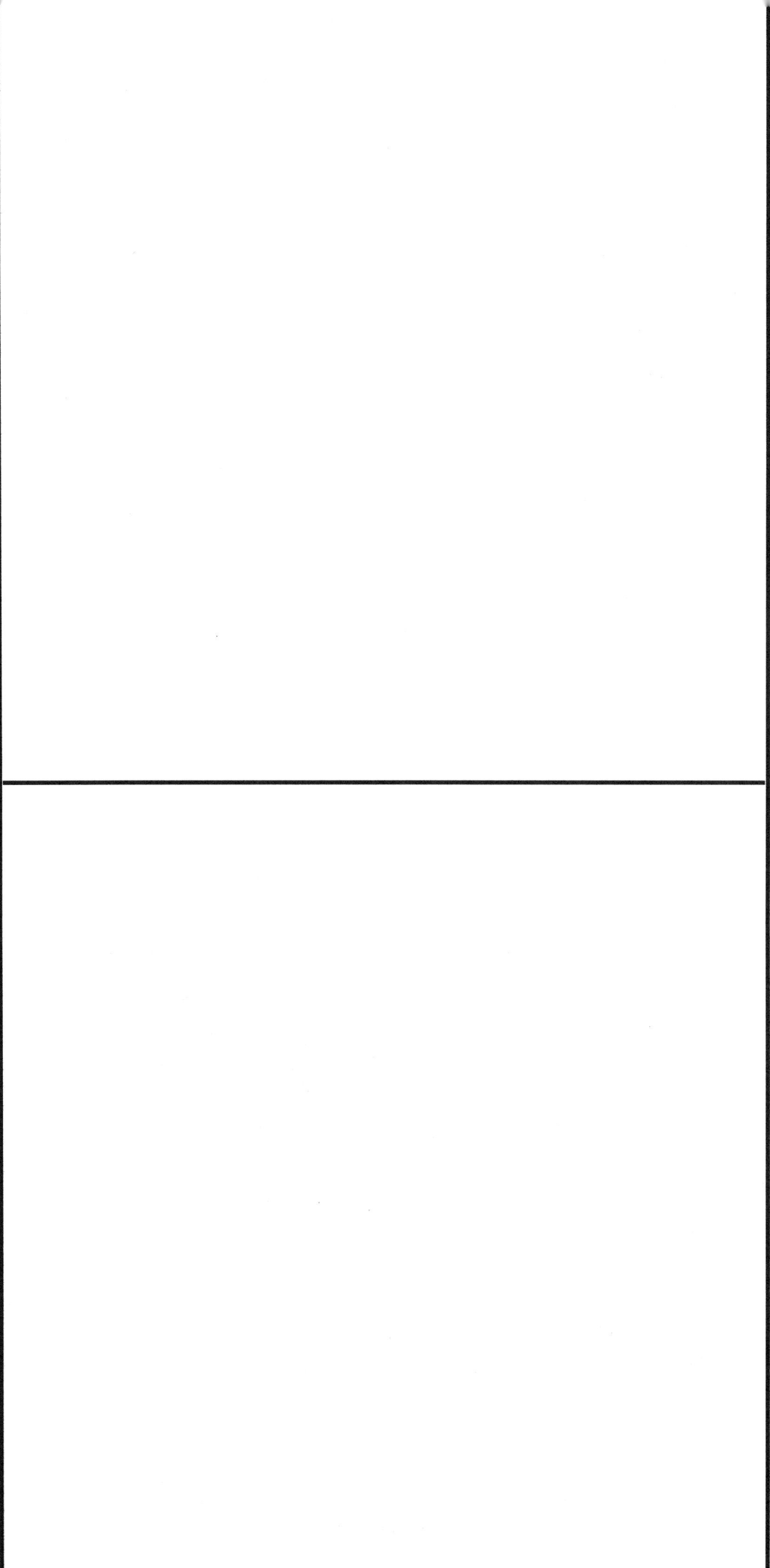

Preparation:
Read Matthew 2:13-23, using the Bible study notes to help you.

Lesson Aim:
To teach that God's plan cannot be thwarted.

Lesson Plan

2:15   See Hosea 11:1. The original context refers to Israel as God's son.

2:16   Herod felt tricked because the Wise Men failed to return as he had asked them to (vv.8,12). The action ordered by Herod fits in with what is known about him. There may have been only a score or so of children of that age in the region, which would explain why there is no record of this by secular historians of the day.

2:17-18   Jeremiah 31:15.

2:22   Archelaus succeeded his father in Judea, Samaria and Idumea. He was seen to be as great a threat as Herod.

Antipas was put in charge of Galilee and Perea.

2:23   Thought to be from Isaiah 11:1 (neser = branch).

Talk to the children about the way things we plan can be spoilt, e.g. an outing can be spoilt by the weather or by someone being ill. Recap on the previous 3 weeks using a question and answer format. Make sure the children realise who Jesus is and how important he is. If God has planned to save his people through Jesus can someone stop it? Let us see what happened when someone tried to get rid of Jesus. Ask the children to listen carefully so that they can tell you who tried to get rid of Jesus and how God sent the warning to Joseph. Tell the story.

At the end of the story go over the answers to the questions and revise the memory verse.

Visual Aids

Continue with the advent calendar - see visual aids for week 2 on page 10.

Activities / 3 - 5s

Photocopy pages 29 and 30 for each child. Prior to the lesson cut slits along the dotted lines on page 29. Cut out Joseph, Mary and the donkey on a strip from page 30 by cutting along the thick black lines. Cut out the extra strips from page 30 and attach one to each end of the figure strip using sellotape on both sides of the join to enable the strip to move smoothly through the slits. The children colour the picture and the figure strip. Insert each end of the strip through the slits on the main picture. Start with Joseph and Mary as far to the left of the picture as possible. Pull the strip to the right to show them travelling to Egypt.

Activities / 5 - 7s

Each child requires 1 A4 sheet of light blue paper, 1 A4 sheet of green paper and page 28 photocopied on paper.

Prior to the lesson:

- With the light blue paper in landscape position, write along the top, 'God told Joseph in a dream to take the baby Jesus to safety in Egypt'.

- Cut the sheet of green paper in half lengthways and save 1 half. Cut a strip 1 cm. wide from the long side of the remaining half and save. Cut 2 hills from the remaining piece (see diagram).

- Write the memory verse along the bottom long side of the saved half sheet of green paper.

- Cut out the figures and rectangle from page 28 and place in an envelope for each child.

Instructions

- Glue the half sheet of green paper onto the blue background, with the memory verse along the bottom.

- Glue the 2 hills above the green paper (see diagram).

- Colour the sign post and glue onto the picture to the right of centre with the base about 6 cm. from the bottom of the page.

- Place the long green strip across the centre of the rectangle labelled X (see diagram). Fold the rectangle along the dotted lines so that it folds around the green strip. Glue the folded sides together to make a conduit through which the green strip can move freely.

- Glue the conduit across the middle of the back of Joseph and Mary (see diagram).

- Glue the 2 ends of the green strip to the picture just below the base of the signpost. Start with Joseph and Mary at the left of the picture and move them along the strip towards Egypt.

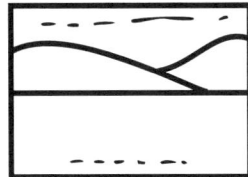

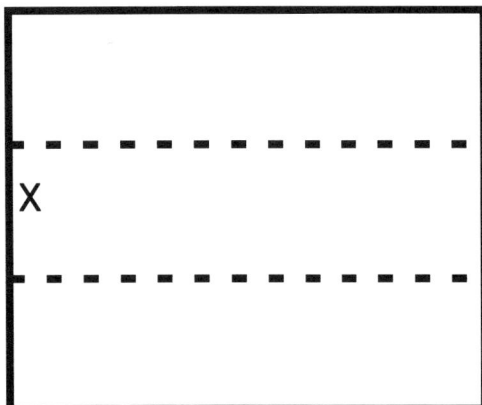

28

Activities / 7 - 9s

Photocopy page 31 for each child. Ask the children to find the following:

- the place where Joseph and Mary lived before Jesus was born (Luke 2:4).
- the town where Jesus was born (Luke 2:6).
- the country where Joseph, Mary and Jesus went to escape from Herod. Draw a line to show the way they might have gone.
- the place where Jesus walked on water (John 6:1,16-21).
- where John baptised Jesus (Matthew 3:13).
- the desert where the Israelites wandered for 40 years (Numbers 14:33-34; 33:15.
- where God gave the 10 commandments to Moses (Exodus 19:2-3).
- 2 places where God dried up water so that the Israelites could cross (Exodus 14:9,15-16, Joshua 3:14-17).

Colour the map if time permits.

Activity for 5-7s

Bethlehem

to Egypt

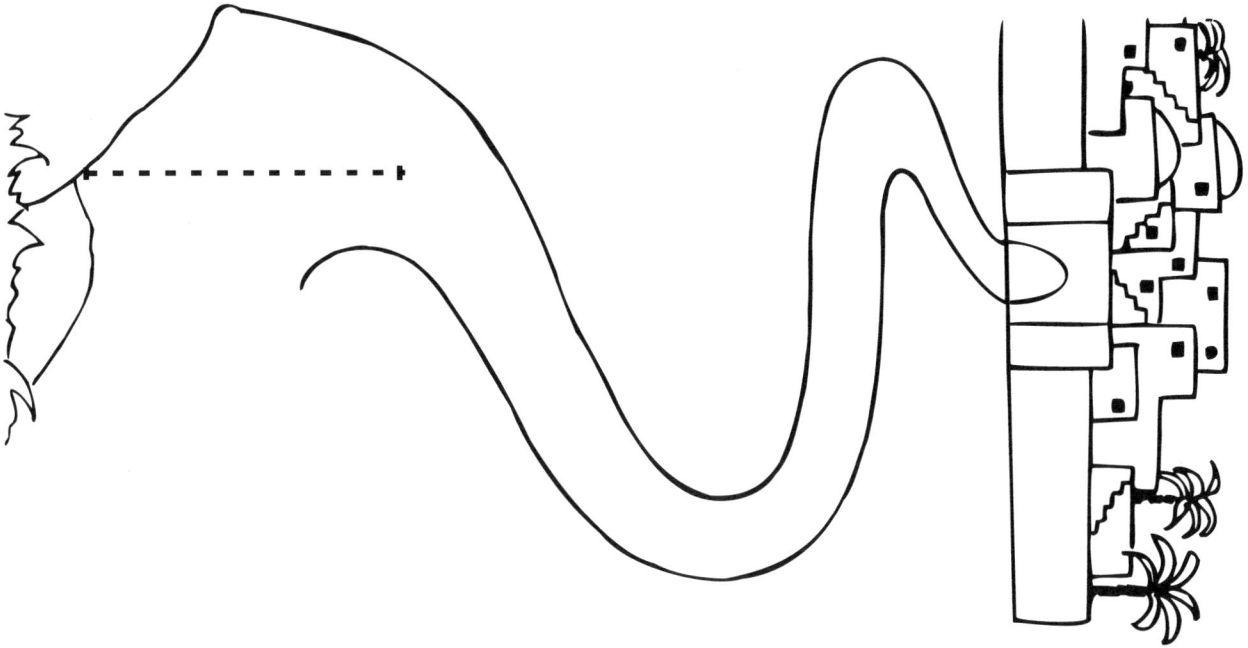

Jesus is the Saviour of the world.
John 4:42

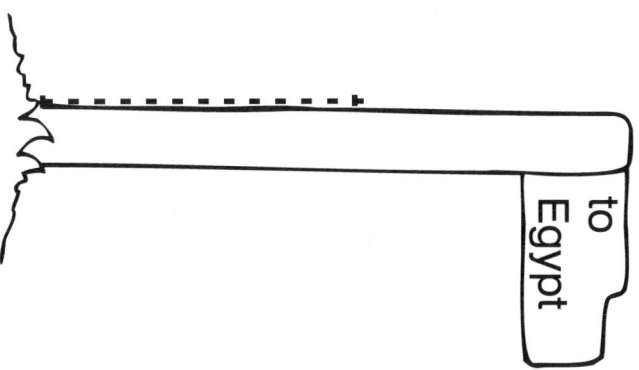

attach to end of strip

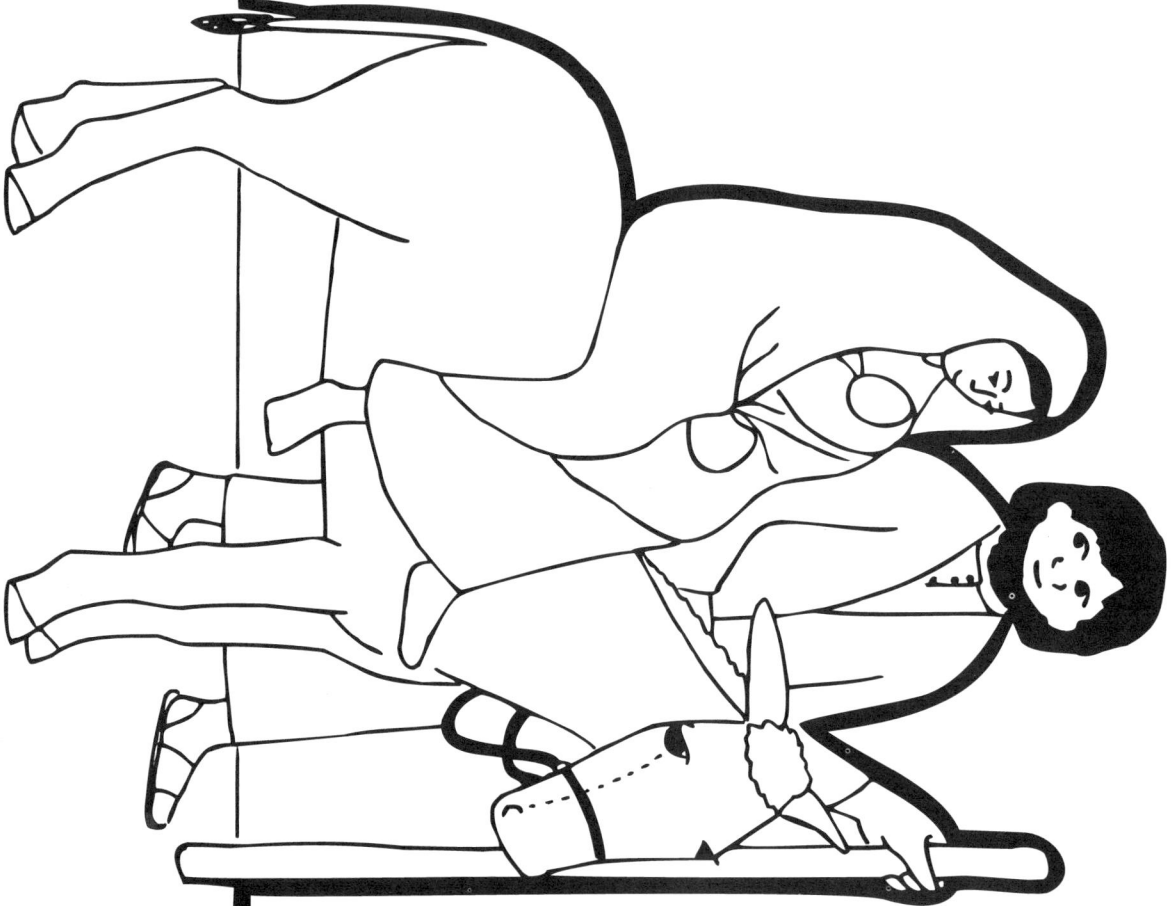

attach to end of strip

30

The Escape to Egypt

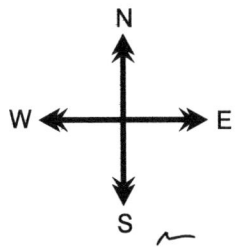

N
W — E
S

Mount Hermon

Sea of Galilee

Nazareth

River Jordan

Mediterranean Sea

Jerusalem

Bethlehem

Dead Sea

Beersheba

Egypt

Sinai Desert

Mount Sinai

River Nile

Red Sea

Jesus Helps......

Overview

Week 6	**JESUS HELPS AT A WEDDING**	*John 2:1-11*

To teach that, as a result of Jesus demonstrating his glory, his followers believed in him.

Week 7	**JESUS HELPS A SICK SON**	*John 4:46-54*

To teach that Jesus' miracles are designed to lead people to faith in him.

Week 8	**JESUS HELPS A CRIPPLED WOMAN**	*Luke 13:10-17*

To show that God is more concerned about the needs of people than about religious rules.

Week 9	**JESUS HELPS TEN LEPERS**	*Luke 17:11-19*

To show the need to associate miracles with God's goodness and be thankful.

Week 10	**JESUS HELPS A BLIND MAN**	*John 9:1-41*

To show that spiritual healing is more important than physical healing.

Series Aims

1. To understand what a miracle is.
2. To understand that the reason for the miracles was to lead people to faith in Jesus as Saviour.

This series looks at 5 of the miracles Jesus performed. A lot of the TV programmes watched by children deal with the fight between good and evil and the supernatural powers possessed by the protagonists. It is important for the children to understand the difference between the miracles of the Bible and the 'supernatural powers' possessed by their cartoon heroes. The miracles show God restoring or creating in line with his nature; they are not random acts of magic (e.g. turning people into frogs).

Miracles A miracle (sign and wonder) takes place when God acts in the natural order in an unusual manner. Its occurrence is predicted and/or takes place at the command or prayer of God's messenger. Miracles are signs that God is at work - they suggest a deeper truth than is at first obvious, and their very strangeness arrests attention. They authenticate the ministry of the person performing them. They are designed to lead the observer(s) to faith in God and to deepen the faith of the believers (John 20:30-31). True miracles always harmonise with the rest of Scripture in their portrayal of God's character.

Miracles are not necessarily a sign that the performer is a Christian (Matthew 7:22-23; 24:24) and, of themselves, do not result in faith in God (John 2:23-25; 9:13-16). One of the problems is that any miracle can be interpreted in different ways, according to the viewpoint of the observers (Matthew 12:22-24).

Jesus' miracles
1. Were brought about by word (Luke 7:6-10) or, in some instances, touch (John 9:6).
2. Brought glory to God (Luke 7:16).
3. Testified to God's love for suffering humanity (Luke 17:11-14).
4. Fulfilled OT prophecies (Luke 7:22 cf. Isaiah 29:18-19; 35:5-6; 61:1).
5. Authenticated his ministry (John 2:11).
6. Demonstrated that he is God. Jesus did things on his own authority, the prophets did things on God's authority (John 4:50, Luke 13:12, cf. 1 Kings 17:1,14-15,20-22, Acts 3:6-8).
7. Led people to faith (John 4:53).

It is important to remember that Jesus came to tell people the good news (Mark 1:14,35-39). The miracles were of secondary importance and sometimes got in the way (Matthew 12:38-39).

Those teaching the older children should give some thought to their position on modern miracles, in case it is raised in class by the children.

Memory Work

Jesus is the Son of God.
1 John 4:15

Preparation:
Read John 2:1-11, using the Bible study notes to help you.

Lesson Aim:
To teach that, as a result of Jesus demonstrating his glory, his followers

In the previous chapter Jesus has met Nathanael, who, after some scepticism, believes that Jesus is the Son of God. Jesus then tells him he will see greater things. Two days later Jesus and his disciples are at Cana (Nathanael's home town, John 21:2) and there he performs his first miracle.

2:1   Cana was about 2-3 days' journey from where John was baptising.

2:3   It would be considered an act of discourtesy for an eastern host not to provide wine for his guests. The incident therefore was not just an inconvenience but a social disaster.

2:4   Jesus was not there to take his direction from Mary. His commands came only from the Father.

2:11   This is called the first of Jesus' signs (miracles). The sign pointed them towards Jesus' identity, leading them into

a recognition of his glory. His very presence and the authority of his teaching had already attracted the disciples to follow him. Having witnessed this manifestation of Jesus' power, the disciples were led into a deeper faith.

Summary In the OT, prophets would point to the glory of God. Here it is Jesus' **own** glory that is manifest, thus the presence of God was being clearly indicated. The disciples responded by believing in Jesus.

Lesson Plan

This is the first of 5 lessons on some of Jesus' miracles which demonstrate that Jesus is truly God.

For the younger children show a series of pictures of individual children and adults. Ask the children to match up children with their parents. How do they know which child goes with which parent (family likeness)? How do we know that Jesus is God? We cannot see him or see God the Father. Jesus does something only God can do. Ask the children to listen carefully so that they can tell you what Jesus did that only God can do.

For the older children prepare 2 identical sets of cards for a famous persons quiz. Each piece of card contains either a question or the name of the person,
e.g.   who was a baby in the reeds in Egypt?
     Moses

The cards can include secular as well as Bible figures and must include the following question about Jesus.
     Who was just like his father?
     Jesus

Split the group into two and give each group a set of cards. The groups compete to see which one can match up the questions and people first. At the end

ask which person stands out from all the rest. Jesus did many wonderful things that showed he is God. Today we will hear about the first one. Ask the children to listen carefully so that they can tell you what the miracle showed about Jesus and how his disciples responded.

After the story go over the answers to the questions and teach the memory verse. Use the story to explain what a miracle is and why they were performed (see the series overview on page 32).

Visual Aids

Make a wedding scene. The backdrop can be made from cardboard or a cardboard box. You need a table with a cloth and food, yoghurt pot people and 6 jars. Jars can either be made from playdough or cardboard cut-outs.

Yoghurt pot people
Requirements
Yoghurt pots or plastic drinking cups, egg cartons, scraps of material, wool, rubber bands, cotton wool, sellotape, glue, pens.

Instructions
Cut the head from an egg carton and sellotape onto a yoghurt pot or plastic cup. Draw on a face. Dress with a piece of material secured round the middle with wool or a rubber band. Tuck the bottom edge of the material inside the bottom of the pot. Attach the head-dress in similar fashion to the robe. Glue on cotton wool as a beard if required.

Activities / 3 - 5s

Photocopy pages 35 and 36 for each child. Prior to the lesson cut out the retaining strip and the strip labelled *water and wine*. Cut along the thick black line around the front jar on page 36 so that the jar will fold up along the dotted line to show the contents. Cut the retaining strip in half and sellotape to the back of page 36 to make slots for the water/wine strip to feed through (see diagram). The

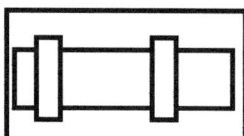

children colour the picture and colour the water section on the strip blue and the wine section red. Slot the strip in place on the back of page 36 with the water visible in the front jar. Ask the children to open the flap to see what is in the jar. Close the flap and move the strip until the wine is in place. Open the flap to show the wine. Make sure that the children understand that Jesus could do this because he is God.

Activities / 5 - 7s

Make a wedding scene. Photocopy pages 37 and 38 on card for each child. Prior to the lesson cut off the hatched areas from page 38. Score and fold along the dotted lines. Cut out the portico, score and fold along the dotted lines. Cut out the figures and bend the tabs backwards. The children colour the figures and make up the model.

Instructions
- The background. Fold along the dotted lines and glue the tabs to the sides.
- Portico. Fold the tabs backwards and glue in place on the background with the Bible verse facing front (see diagram).
- Glue the figures in the places marked on the background with the tabs facing the back.

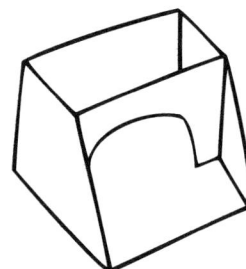

Activities / 7 - 9s

Over the next 5 weeks the children will make a book. Do not send home until it is finished (week 10). Photocopy page 39 on card and pages 40, 41 and 42 on paper for each child. Each child also requires an A4 slide binder and an A4 sheet of card for the back cover. Prior to the story answer the questions on page 40. Page 41 is for use after the story to reinforce the reasons for the miracle. Page 42 is done last.

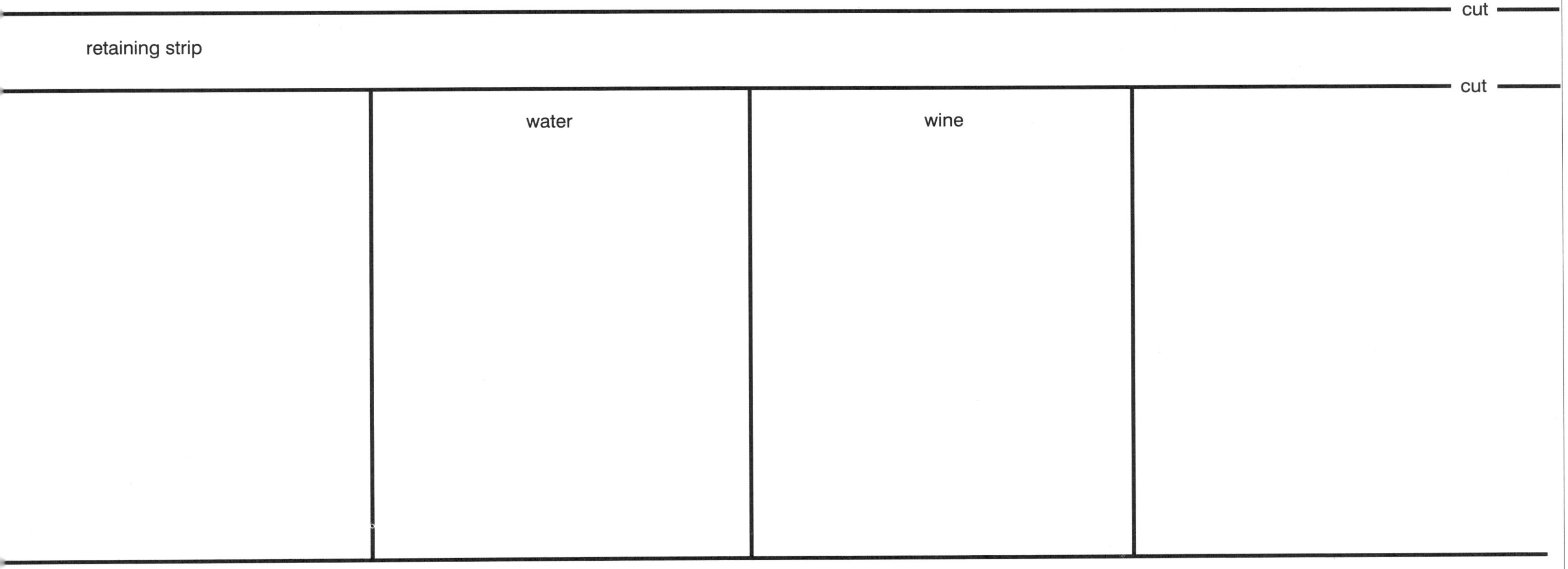

retaining strip

water

wine

cut

cut

35

Jesus was a guest at a wedding. Part way through the feast they ran out of wine. Open the flap to see what Jesus did.

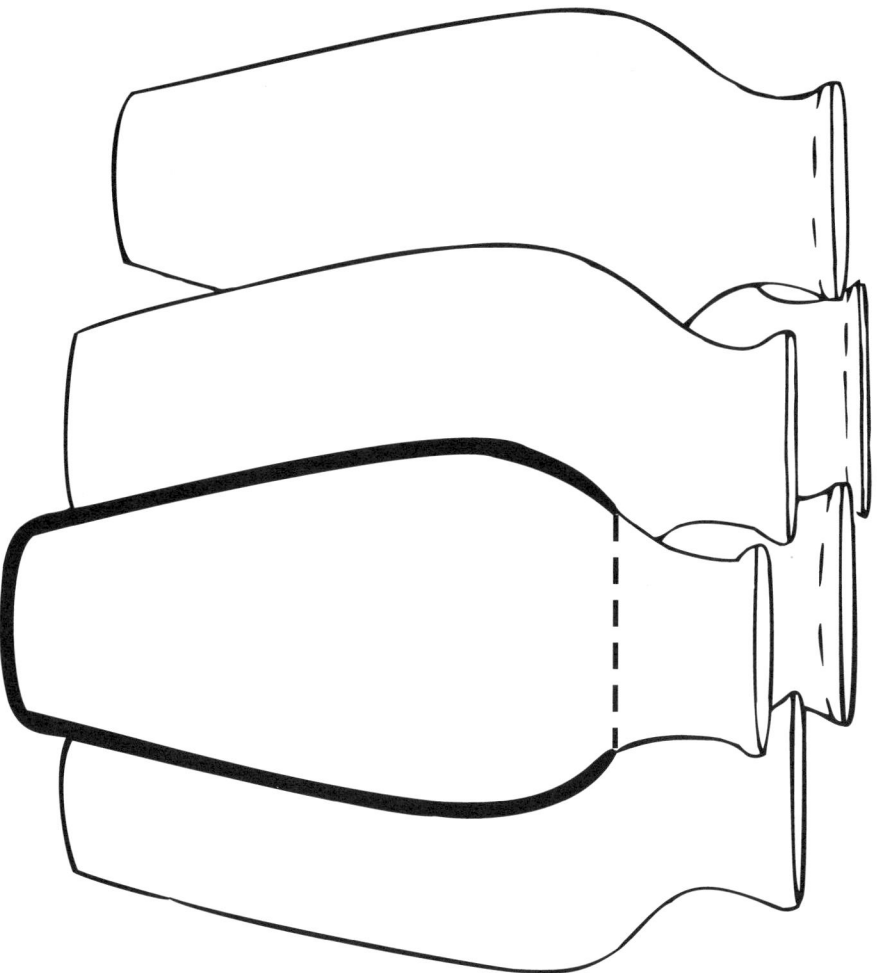

Jesus is the
Son of God.

1 John 4:15

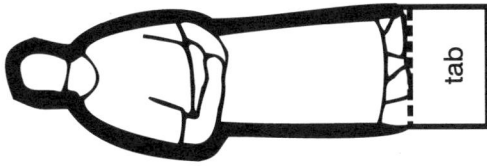

slave

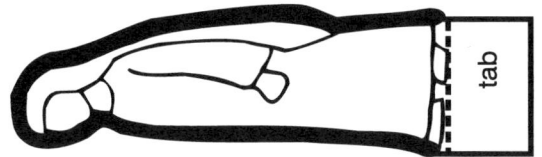

Mary

tab

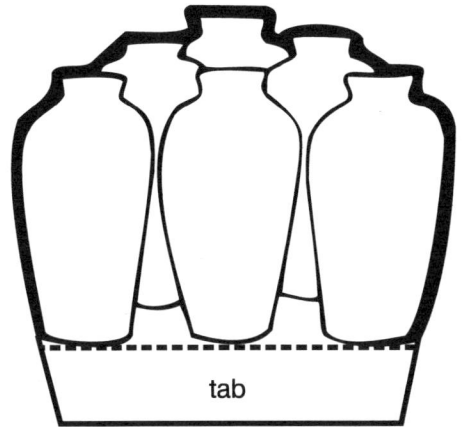

tab

portico

Jesus is the Son of God.   1 John 4:15

tab

tab

cut out
and discard

discard

tab

tab

discard

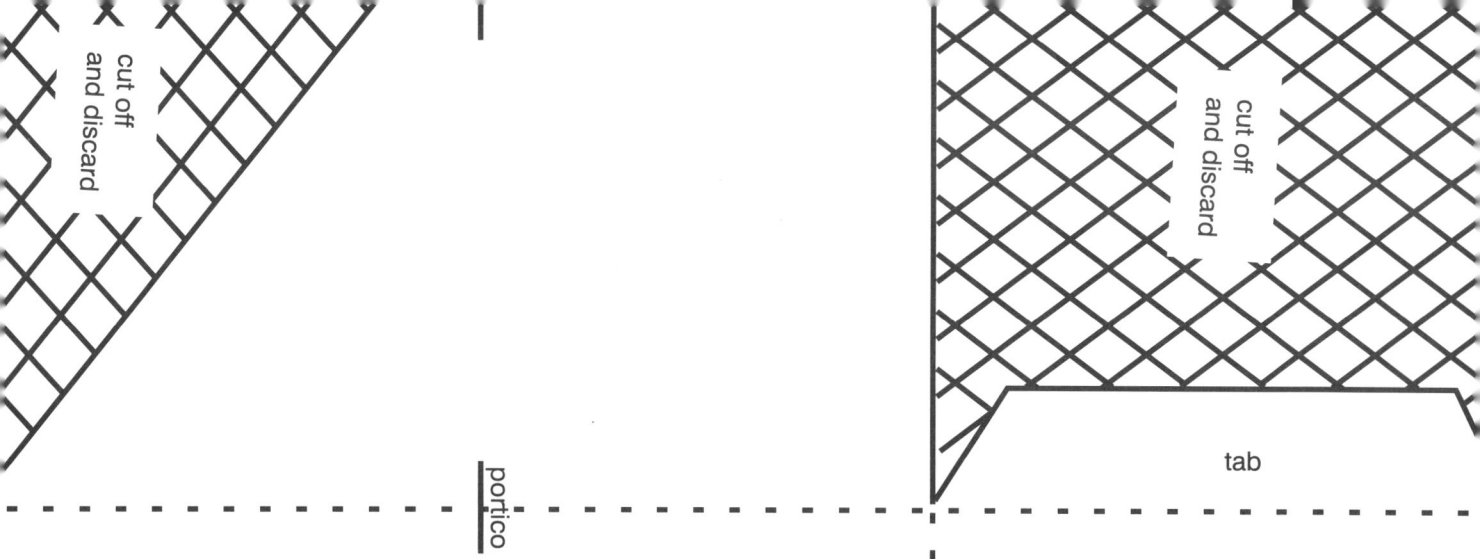

cut off and discard

cut off and discard

tab

portico

slave

Mary

wedding party

jars

portico

tab

cut off and discard

cut off and discard

cut off and discard

38

Name ....

A miracle takes place when God causes something to happen that would not have otherwise happened.

Were the following happenings miracles?

The plague of locusts	☐ yes	☐ no
The giving of the 10 commandments	☐ yes	☐ no
The fall of Jericho	☐ yes	☐ no
Elijah fed by the ravens	☐ yes	☐ no
Esther chosen as queen	☐ yes	☐ no

Jesus did many miracles.
Look up John 20:31 to discover the main reasons for Jesus' miracles.

To show that Jesus is the Son of God	☐ yes	☐ no
To show that Jesus was a great teacher	☐ yes	☐ no
To show that Jesus was the best doctor	☐ yes	☐ no
To help me believe in Jesus	☐ yes	☐ no
To help me to do the things that Jesus did	☐ yes	☐ no

Did everyone who saw Jesus do miracles believe that he was the Messiah, the Son of God?
(Look up John 9:13-16)   ☐ yes   ☐ no

Jesus Helps ...

at a wedding.   John 2:1-11

What was the problem?

☐ no food

☐ no wine

☐ no water

What miracle did Jesus perform?

☐ fed 5,000 people

☐ turned water into wine

☐ brought water out of the rock

What did this miracle reveal about Jesus?

☐ he knew what men were thinking

☐ he cared if people were hungry

☐ his glory

What was the result?

☐ people had enough to eat

☐ everyone believed in him

☐ his disciples believed in him

Should I expect God to perform a miracle to get me out of a difficult situation?

Memory Verse Puzzle

Why was Jesus able to turn water into wine? To find out, start with the letter J in the upper left-hand corner of the water jar and follow the lines, using every letter once only. Put arrow marks on the lines so that you can see where you have been. Write the letters in the spaces below the water jar. End with the letter v in the bottom right-hand corner. The first 2 arrows have been put in to help you get started.

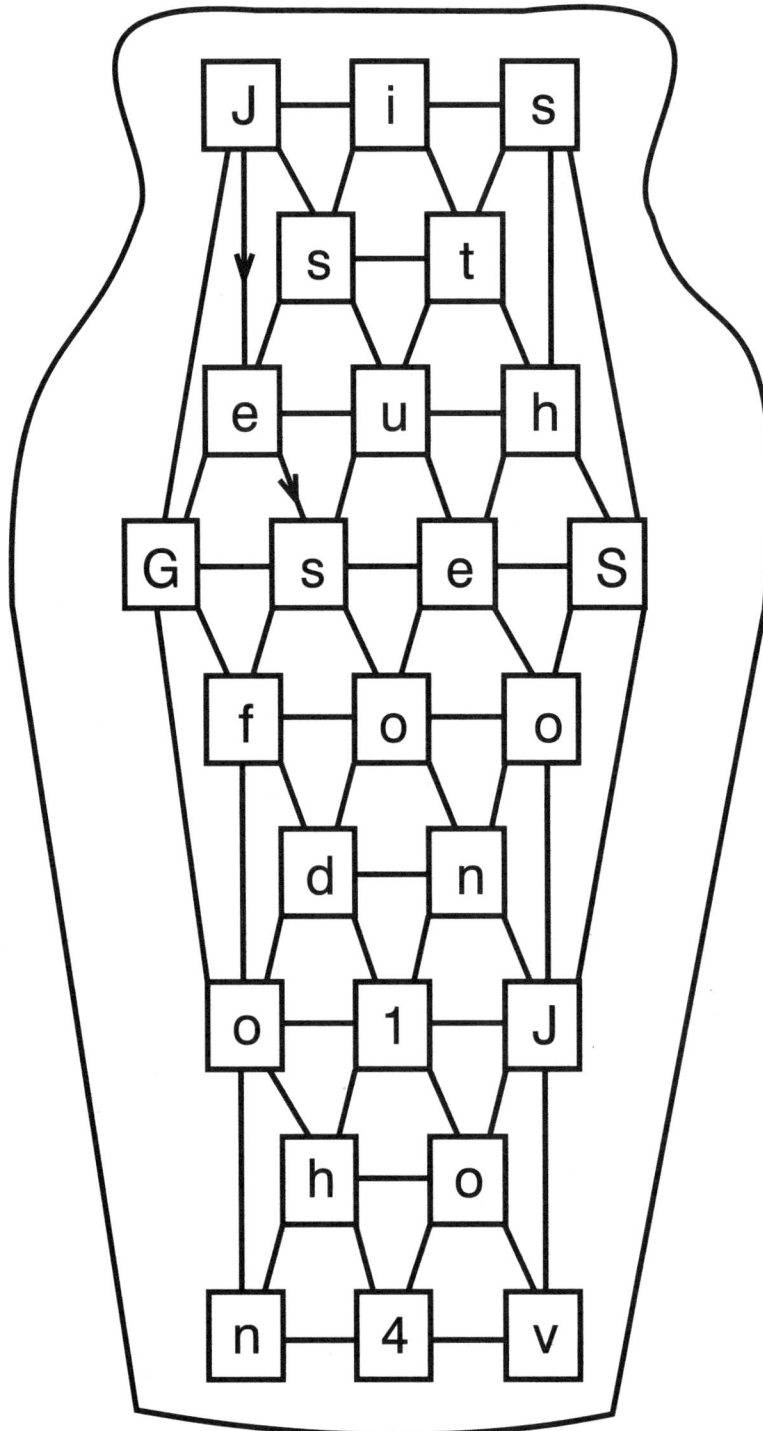

_ .

_ _ _ _ _ _ _

Preparation:

Read John 4:46-54, using the Bible study notes to help you.

Lesson Aim:

To teach that Jesus' miracles are designed to lead people to faith in him.

This is the second recorded sign (miracle) in John's gospel and again it takes place in Cana, the home of Nathanael (John 1:47-51).

4:46   This person was probably an official in the court of Herod Antipas, described as King of Galilee. Capernaum was 25 miles from Cana.

4:47-48   Jesus reads the character of the man. He seems to show faith, but it is a faith that needs the support of sight, i.e. Jesus going with him, unlike the centurion in Luke 7:1-10.

4:49-50   The faith of the man is, however, imperfect; desperate for his child not to die he persists in asking Jesus for healing. Jesus says to him, 'Go, your son will live.' He returns home in obedience to Jesus' words, trusting that his son will be healed. Now he does not require to see anything - he believes.

4:51-53   The healing was immediate and complete. It happened at the very hour Jesus had said that the boy would live. This sign led to belief in Jesus, not only for the man but his entire family.

NB Our faith and the children's can start in a small way, but as we learn more and more and are challenged to exercise it, our faith in the Lord should become stronger and stronger.

Lesson Plan

Start with a game to demonstrate trust.

Game 1 Mark out a route containing obstacles that could be bumped into or tripped over. Ask for a volunteer who trusts a designated leader to lead them safely through the obstacle course. Blindfold the volunteer. The volunteer is led through the obstacle course accompanied by comments from another leader, e.g. 'Be careful!' 'You're going to hit .....', etc.

Game 2 Ask for a volunteer who trusts 2 designated leaders to keep him/her safe. Blindfold the volunteer and explain he/she is going on an aeroplane ride. Sit the volunteer between the 2 leaders, holding onto them. The volunteer is told to hold on tight. A leader states that the plane is taking off and the 2 leaders pull the volunteer slightly backwards against the chair. A running commentary of a plane ride is given with the 2 leaders moving the volunteer appropriately. At some point the commentator calls out, 'Watch out! You'll hit the ceiling!' and one of the leaders lightly touches the top of the volunteer's head with a book. Then the 'plane' is brought down to land.

Lead into the story by commenting on the volunteer's trust (or lack of it). How do we know the volunteer trusted the leader(s)? He/she did what they said. In today's true story from the Bible we will learn about a man who said he trusted Jesus. Ask the children to listen carefully so that they can tell you who was the

man, what he trusted Jesus to do and how we know he really trusted Jesus. Tell the story.

After the story go over the answers to the questions. Recap on what a miracle is and ask the older children what miracles teach about the person performing them. Revise the memory verse.

Visual Aids

Yoghurt pot people (see instructions on page 34). Make a bed from a piece of material. The children need to see that Jesus and the father were at a distance from the son when he was healed, so have Jesus and the father at one end of the table or room and the son on a bed at the other end.

Activities / 3 - 5s

Photocopy pages 45 and 46 for each child. Prior to the lesson cut out the son and the square from page 45 and cut around 3 sides of the window flap on page 46, leaving the dotted line intact. The children colour the picture, the bed and the son. Attach the son to the bed using a split pin paper fastener at X. Glue the bed square behind page 46 so that the bed is visible through the window. The children can lift the flap to see the son sick in bed, then turn him upright when he is made well.

Activities / 5 - 7s

Photocopy pages 47 and 48 for each child. Prior to the lesson cut out the hatched areas on page 48 and cut off the retaining strip and the figures strip from page 47. Cut along the dotted lines on page 48. From the back of the picture feed the figure strip through the two slits on the house. Place the retaining strip over the figure strip and sellotape to the back of the picture so that the figures on the strip will be visible in the house (see diagram). The

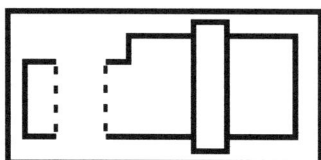

children colour the picture and the figures on the strip. Slot the figure strip in place on the back of the picture with the boy visible lying on his bed. Point out what the father is saying. Pull the strip until the words of Jesus appear in the other speech bubble. Point out what has happened to the boy. Remind the children that the boy got better at the very time that Jesus said, 'Your son will live!' (v.53).

Activities / 7 - 9s

Continue with the activity book. Photocopy page 49 on paper and page 50 on card for each child. The decoded question is, 'Do we need to see a miracle before we can believe in Jesus?' Use this to discuss the importance of true faith in Jesus, i.e. faith that is not propped up with signs and wonders (v.48). Attach page 49 to the back of the book.

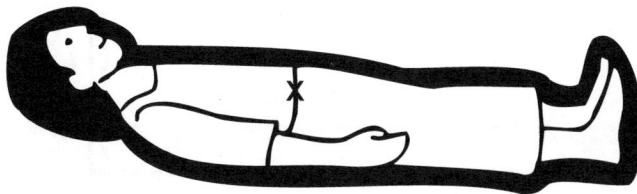

Jesus is the Son of God.   1 John 4:15

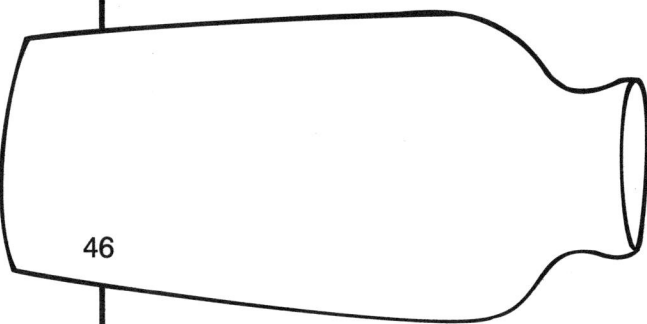

46

Go, your son will live!

Come before my child dies.

retaining strip

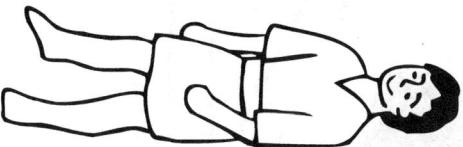

A father came to Jesus to ask him to heal his son. Pull the slider to see what Jesus did.

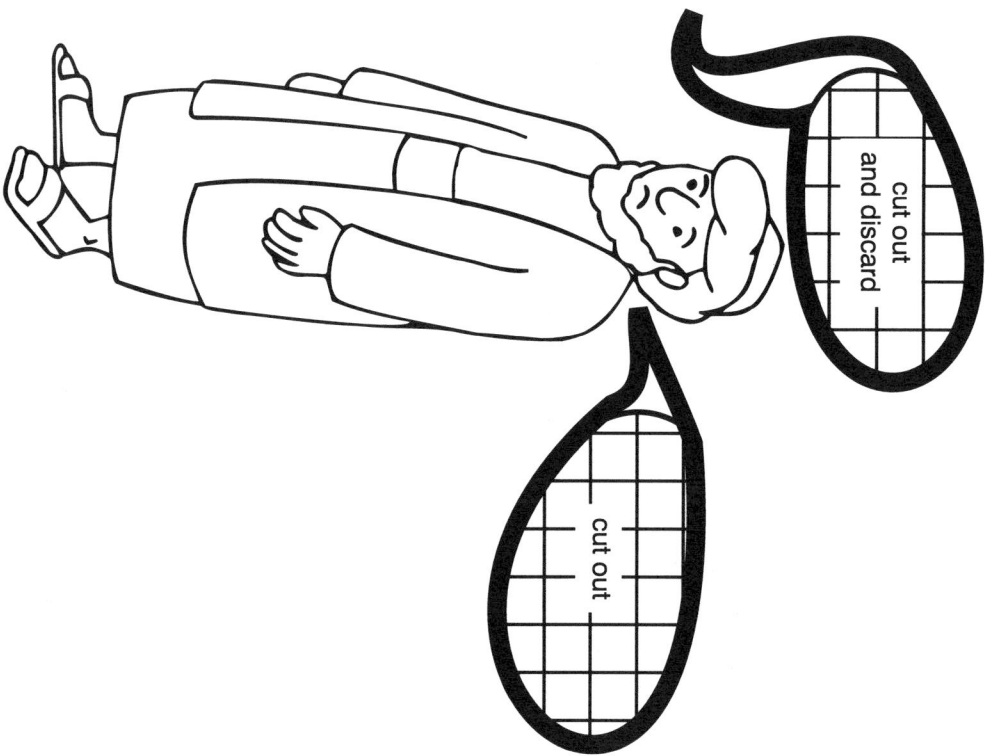

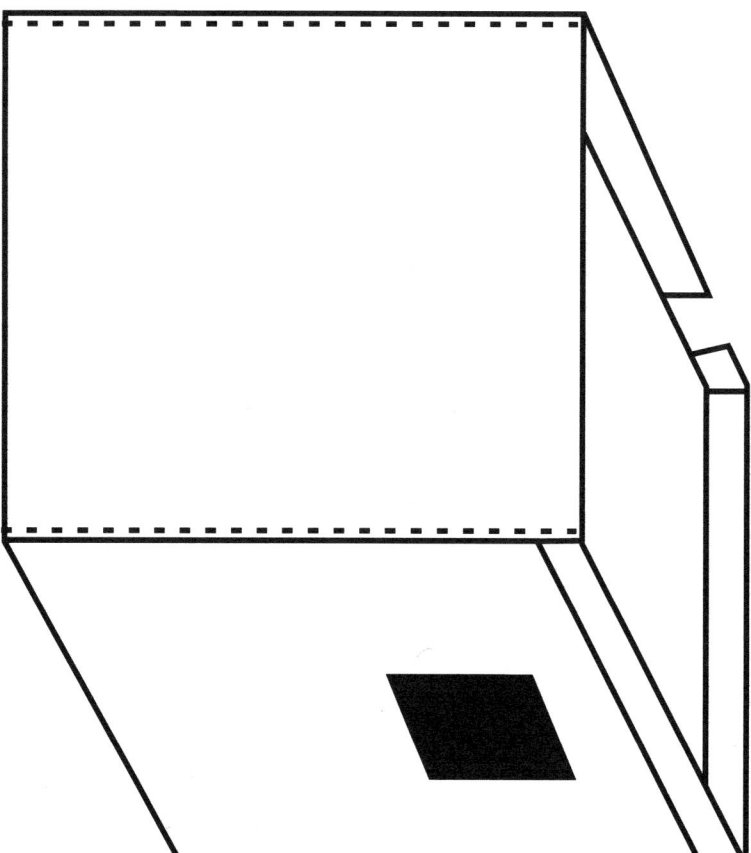

cut out
and discard

cut out

Jesus is the Son of God.
1 John 4:15

Jesus Helps ...

a sick son. John 4:46-54

What was the problem?

☐ the son was mildly ill

☐ the son was about to die

☐ the son was dead

What did Jesus do about it?

☐ he told the father to have faith in him

☐ he went to the father's house

☐ he said, 'your son will live'

How did the man show he believed Jesus?

☐ he did what Jesus said

☐ he promised to be a follower of Jesus

☐ he bowed down and worshipped Jesus

What was the result?

☐ the father believed

☐ the whole family believed

☐ the disciples believed

Make your decoder and use it to discover the last question.

x c   r m   t m m x   i c   k m m n   q l g n f w m

v m y c g m   r m   f n t   v m w l m a m l t   p m k o k   ?

Outer disc letters: V Z O K H C R Q T Y S I E A U J M W P N G B L D F X

Inner disc letters: a b c d e f g h i j k l m n o p q r s t u v w x y z

Find the letter in the hole on the inner dial. The arrow will point to the letter you need to decode your message.

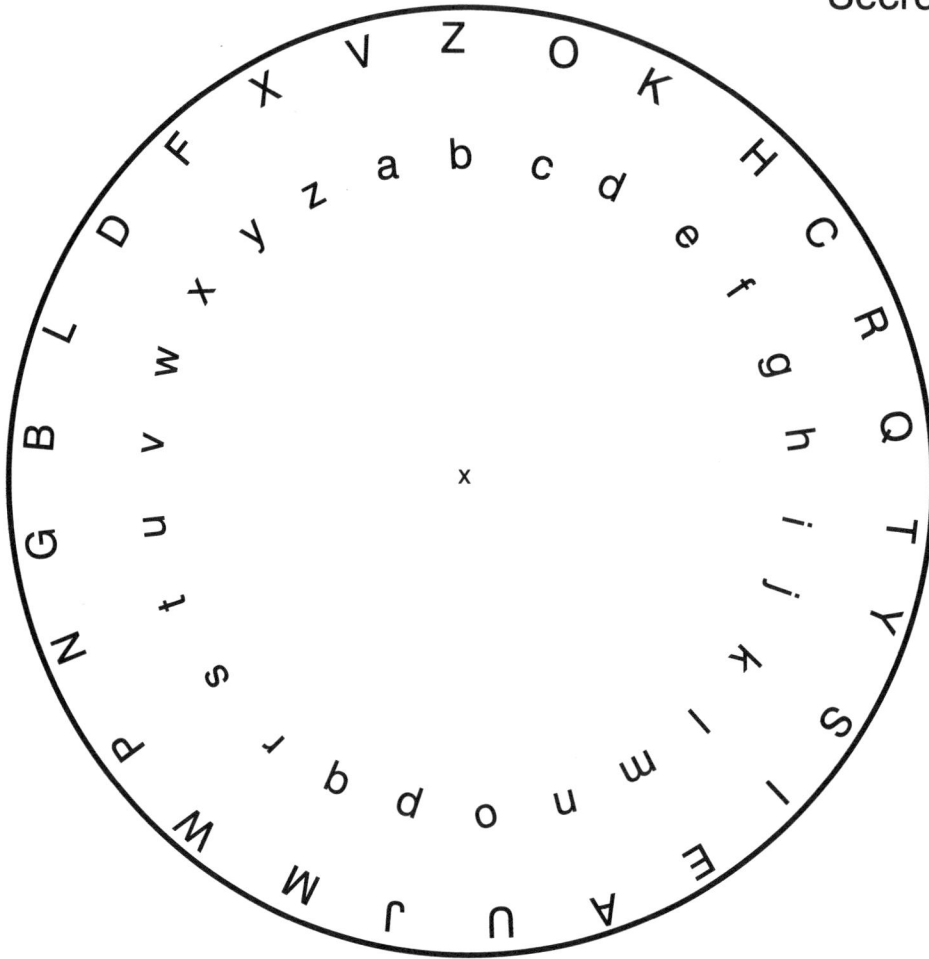

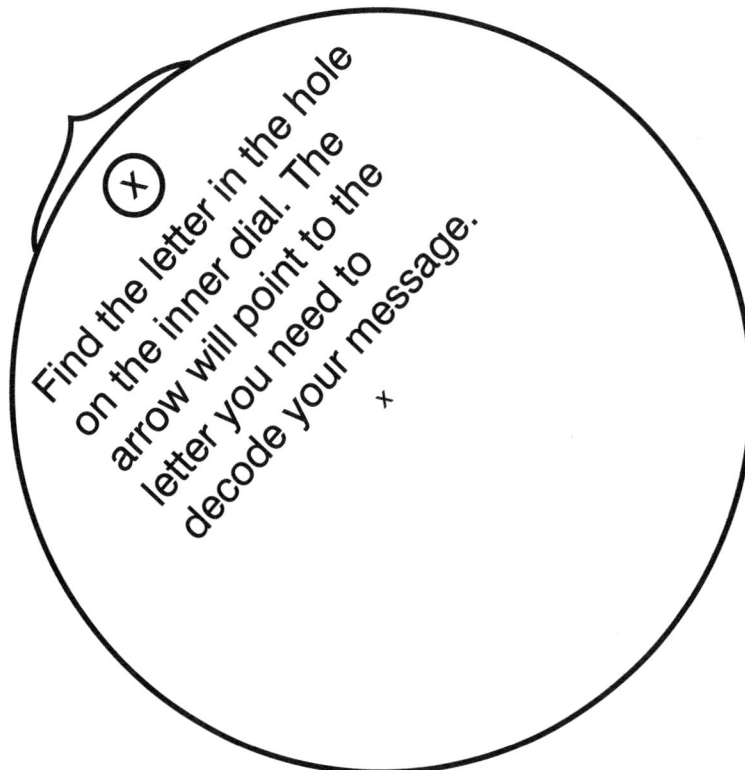

Cut out both discs. Punch a hole at ⊗ Attach the small disc on top of the big disc using a split pin paper fastener through the centres. Make sure that the 2 discs can rotate independently.

Jesus Helps a Crippled Woman

Preparation:

Read Luke 13:10-17, using the Bible study notes to help you.

Lesson Aim:

To show that God is more concerned about the needs of people than about religious rules.

13:17   'All the people were delighted', (Greek - 'kept rejoicing'), about all the wonderful things Jesus had done.

Lesson Plan

13:10   This is the last recorded time Jesus taught in a synagogue and was not long before he started his final journey to Jerusalem.

13:11   The woman had a spinal deformity.

13:12   She did not come to Jesus. He took the initiative.

13:15-16   The woman's illness was due to Satan's activity from which she must be loosed. The woman was attending the synagogue. The rabbis were greatly concerned for animals. On the Sabbath an animal could be led on a lead but not carried. It could be given water to drink from a trough but a bucket could not be held for the animal. If it was acceptable to free animals to be fed on the Sabbath, then how much more should this woman, a member of the family of Israel, be freed to enjoy life to its full.

The introduction aims to demonstrate how difficult every day life would have been for the crippled woman. Ask the younger children to bend over. Give them various tasks to do, e.g. walk around the room, pick up a book from the table, put on a jumper. Explain that they must perform these tasks without straightening up.

For the older children give them 1 minute to act what they have done so far today, e.g. got up, washed, dressed, had breakfast. Then give them 1 minute to do the same tasks bent over.

Ask the children to comment on how difficult they found the tasks when bent over. In today's true story from the Bible we will hear about a lady who had something wrong with her back bone which caused her to be bent over. Ask the children to listen carefully so that they can tell you how Jesus made her better and what the religious leaders thought about it. Tell the story.

After the story go over the answers to the questions and recap on what a miracle is. Have we learnt anything else about miracles in today's story? Revise the memory verse.

Visual Aids

Use stand-up figures. You will need the people in the synagogue, an official, and the woman. Glue the figures onto card and attach a piece of card to the backs to enable them to stand upright (see diagram). The woman needs to be made in 2 halves and joined with a split pin so that she can straighten up.

Activities / 3 - 5s

Make a model of the crippled woman. Each child requires page 53 photocopied on card and 2 pipe cleaners. Prior to the lesson cut out the lady and make a frame for the body using the pipe cleaners (see diagram). The children colour the lady and fold her in half at the dotted line. Place her over the frame and glue or staple the edges together. The lady can be bent over then straightened.

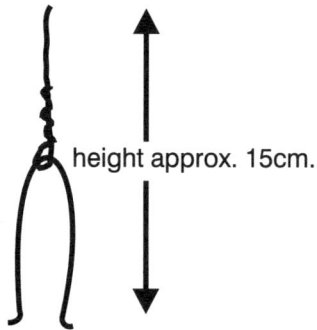

height approx. 15cm.

Activities / 5 - 7s

Make a model of the crippled woman. Photocopy page 54 on card for each child. Prior to the lesson cut off the section containing the woman's body and fold in half along the dotted line. Cut out the body and skirt. Cut the skirt along the fold line to make 2 pieces. Cut out the 2 wheels with feet. The children colour the parts and glue the 2 sides of the body together. Using a split pin paper fastener, attach the body between the top of the 2 skirt sections at X. The body can be bent or straightened. Glue the 2 wheels together back to back and attach between the bottom of the 2 skirt sections using a split pin paper fastener at X (see diagram). Make sure that the wheel moves freely on the pin and that there is enough space between the wheel and the skirt to allow the woman to 'walk' along the table top.

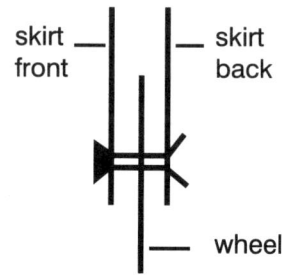

skirt front — skirt back

— wheel

Activities / 7 - 9s

Continue with the activity book. Photocopy page 53 on card and page 55 on paper for each child. Make the woman before the story, following the instructions for the 3-5s, and use as a visual aid. Attach page 55 to the back of the book.

Jesus is the Son of God. 1 John 4:15

The Blind Man   Activity for 3-5s

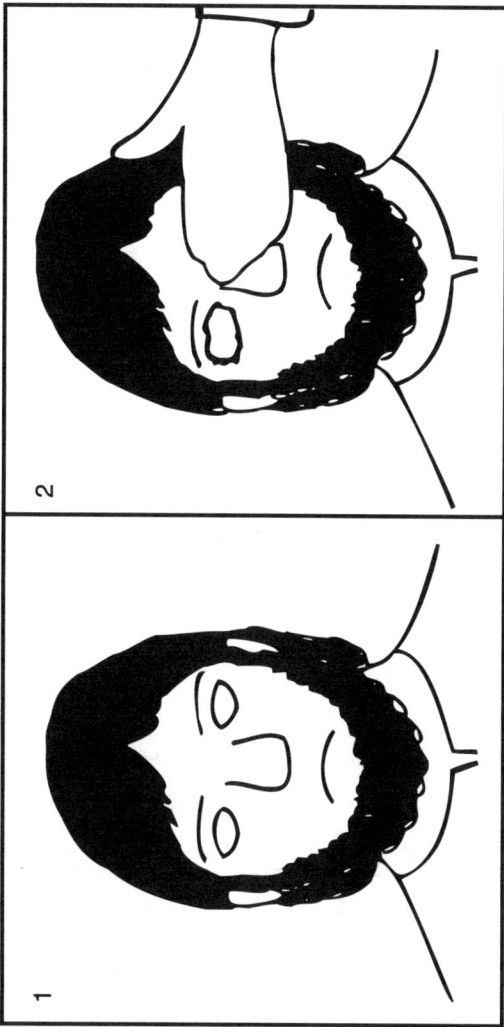

2

1

53

 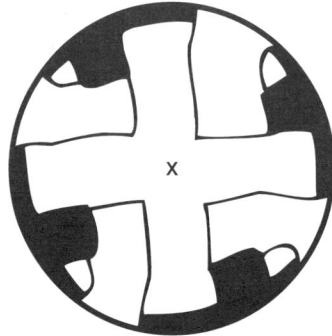

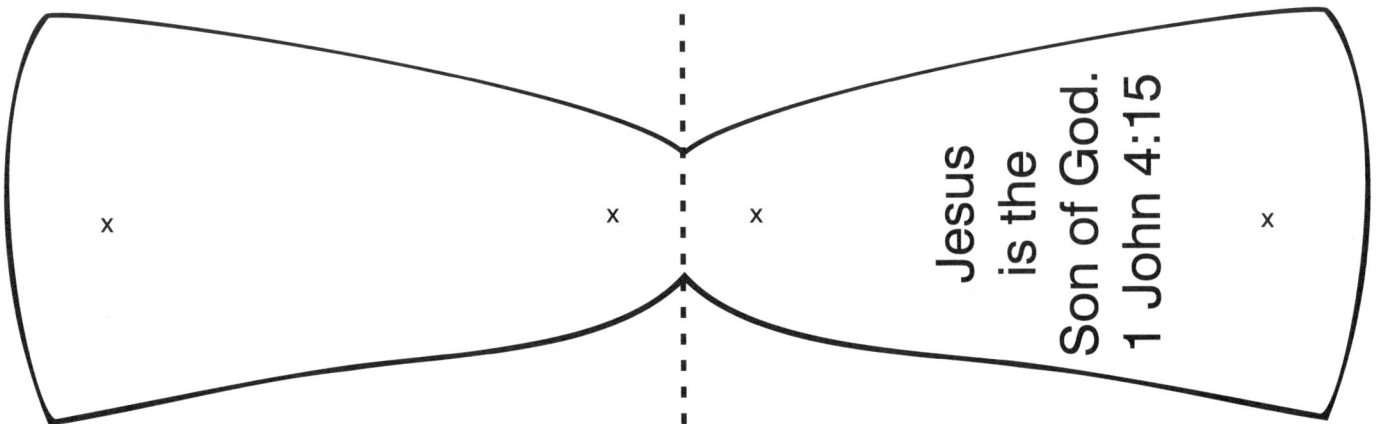

Jesus
is the
Son of God.
1 John 4:15

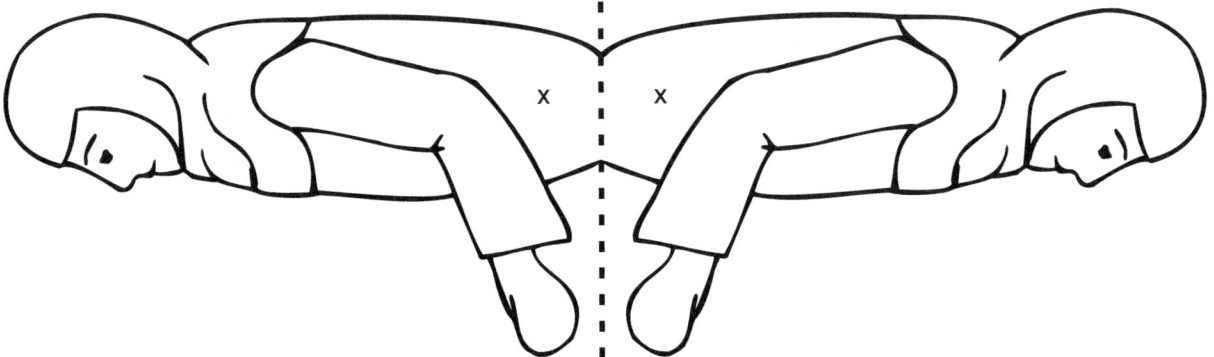

Jesus Helps ...

a crippled woman.   Luke 13:10-17

What was the problem?
The woman could not straighten up because an evil spirit had made her ill for

8 years   ☐

10 years   ☐

18 years   ☐

How did Jesus heal her?

☐   with a word

☐   with a touch

☐   by washing in a pool

Was the woman healed because of her faith in Jesus?   ☐ yes

☐ no

What was the result of the miracle?

☐   the woman praised God

☐   the ruler of the synagogue praised God

☐   all the people rejoiced

What have you learnt about miracles so far in this series?

Jesus performed miracles to show who he was	☐ yes	☐ no
The person had to have faith in Jesus	☐ yes	☐ no
Jesus always healed people the same way	☐ yes	☐ no
The people who saw the miracle ended up believing in Jesus	☐ yes	☐ no

Jesus Helps Ten Lepers

Preparation:
Read Luke 17:11-19, using the Bible study notes to help you.

Lesson Aim:
To show the need to associate miracles with God's goodness and be thankful.

17:12-13   He met them at the entrance to a village. Lepers were forbidden by the Law to enter a village. They could not come near 'clean' people so they shouted. They asked Jesus to pity them, which was a request for healing.

17:14   He did not touch them or even say, 'You are healed'. He told them to show themselves to the priest. This was the procedure required by the Law for a person who had been cured of leprosy. The priest had to be satisfied that the person had been cured before he/she could return to live within normal society (Leviticus 14:1-3). Their faith was put to the test - they had to act as though they had been healed. As they obeyed, so it happened!

17:15-16   When one of them realised he had been healed he immediately returned to Jesus, thanking him and praising God. He was not afraid to show his joy. When he saw Jesus he acted with humility and bowed down, thanking the master. Normally Jews and Samaritans had little to do with each other, but for those suffering from leprosy some company was better than none! The nine were so absorbed in their new happiness that they could not spare a thought for the one who had helped them. The exception was a foreigner, not one of the chosen people.

17:19   Although the others had faith they would be healed (which was the case in most miracles), this Samaritan had faith **and** was thankful. It is quite possible that 'your faith has made you well' means more than a cure - the Greek means 'has saved you'. He had been given the gift of salvation as well as bodily healing.

NB God's goodness is all around us and is not limited to those who follow Jesus. God has provided us with all the good things that we enjoy. What we learn from this story is that God wants us to enjoy not just his material goodness but also his spiritual blessings, which we have through faith in Jesus. It needs to be borne in mind that healing does not necessarily lead to saving faith. Only one is told that his faith has saved him. The children need to realise that not everyone is thankful for what God has done for us. We need to be!

Lesson Plan

Show the children pictures of several apples and 1 pear. Ask them which is the odd one out. Do this with other items, e.g. furniture, shapes. Finally pin up the 10 lepers (see pages 59 and 60). Which is the odd one out? In today's true story from the Bible we will find out which one is. Ask the children to listen carefully so that they can tell you what made one of the lepers different. The older children can be asked to work out how this healing differed from the previous 2 studied. Tell the story.

After the story go over the answers to the questions and recap on what a miracle is. Revise the memory verse.

Visual Aids

Make a concertina strip of 10 men (see diagram). Separate 1 from the other nine at the point when the 1 comes back to say 'thank you'. Alternatively, use 10 finger puppets.

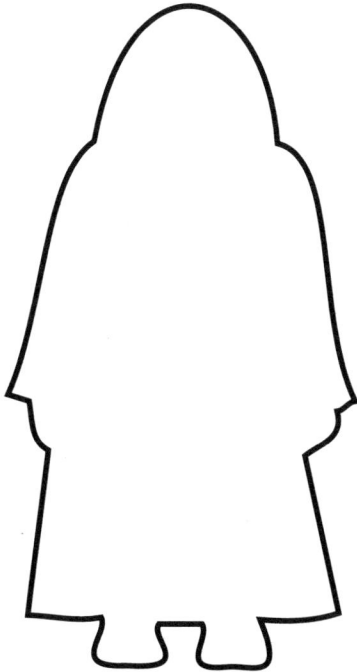

Finger puppets
1. Using the templates (see below), cut out a body and arms. Draw on a face, head-dress, clothes and hands and colour appropriately. The arms and hands should be coloured on both sides.
2. Roll the body into a tube and glue the back together along the dotted area.
3. Glue the arms onto the back of the body (see diagram).

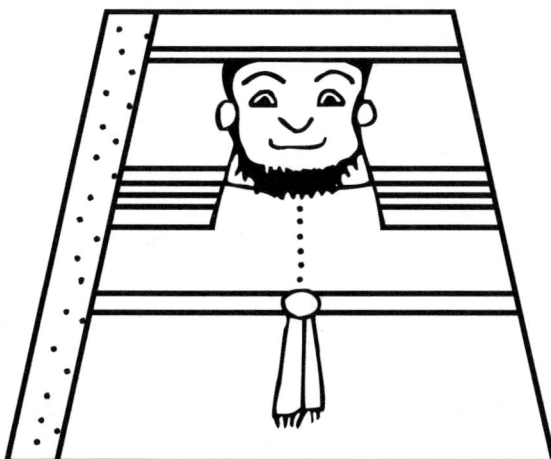

Activities / 3 - 5s

Make a pendant. Photocopy page 58 on card for each child. Prior to the lesson cut out the 2 circles. The children colour the pictures and glue them together so that there is a picture on both sides. Make a hole at X using a hole punch. Thread a piece of wool through the hole and join at the ends. The wool loop must be big enough to go over the child's head.

Activities / 5 - 7s

Photocopy pages 59 and 60 on card for each child. Prior to the lesson cut out the 10 lepers and write 'thank-you' on the back of 1 of them. The children colour the lepers then spread them out in any order on the table. The object of the game is to put the lepers in the order of the memory verse then pick out the one who said, 'Thank-you.'

Make a set for yourself to play the game with the children. Encourage the children to play the game at home with their family.

Activities / 7 - 9s

Continue with the activity book. Photocopy page 61 for each child and add to the back of the book.

Prior to the lesson cut out 10 men from blotting paper (see visual aids diagram). Using the scissors blade rough up the back of each cut-out so that it will stick to a flannelgraph background. Write one word of the memory verse and reference onto each man -

Jesus is the Son of God 1 John 4 15

At the start of the lesson place the men haphazardly on the board and get the children to put them in the right order to test their knowledge of the memory verse.

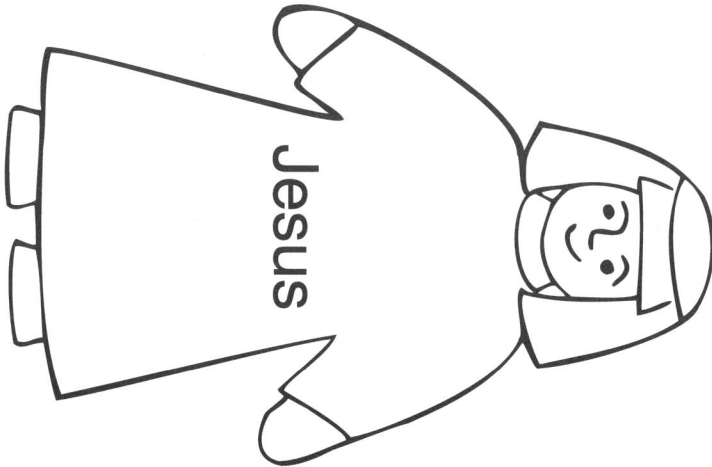

Son

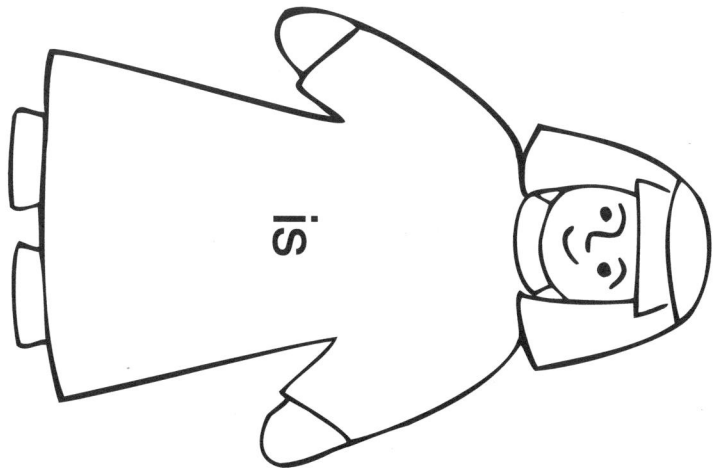

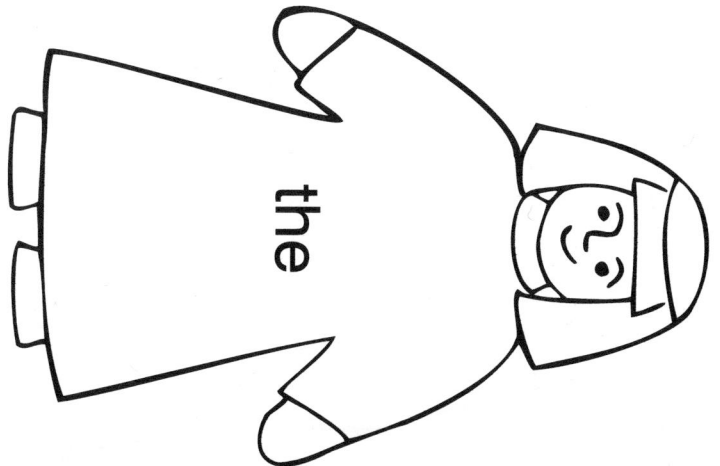

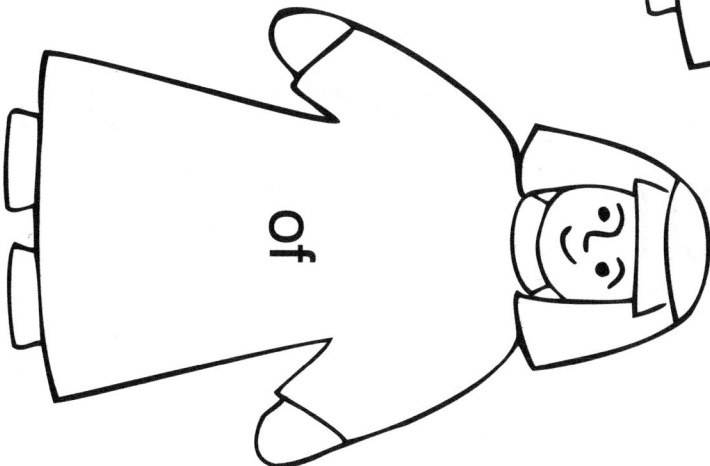

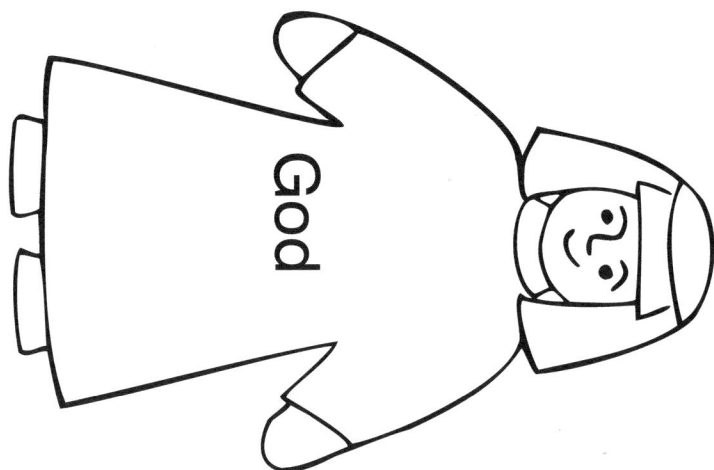

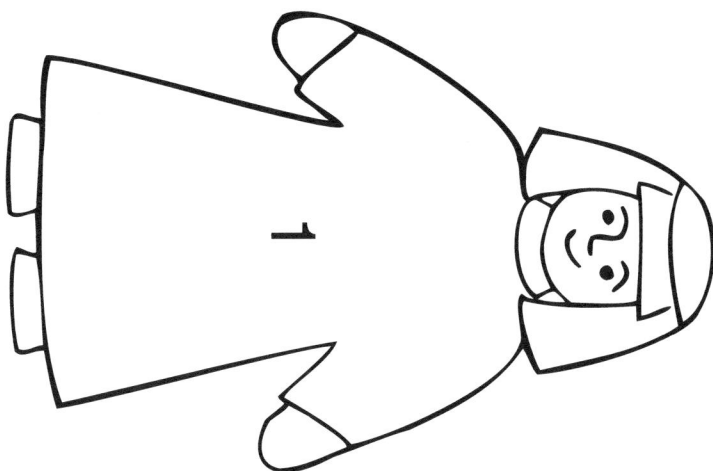

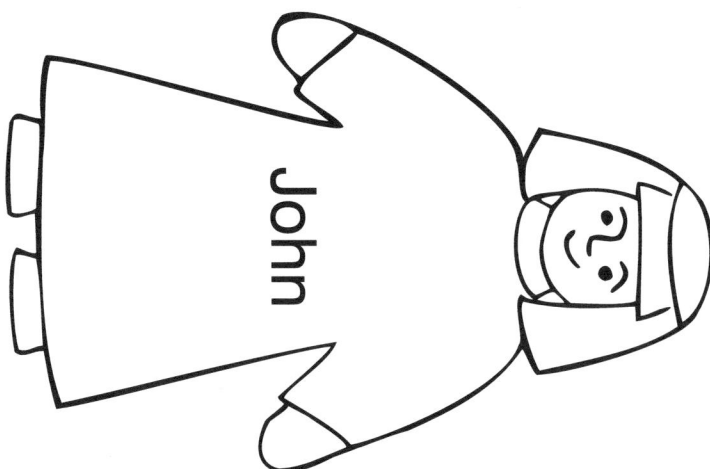

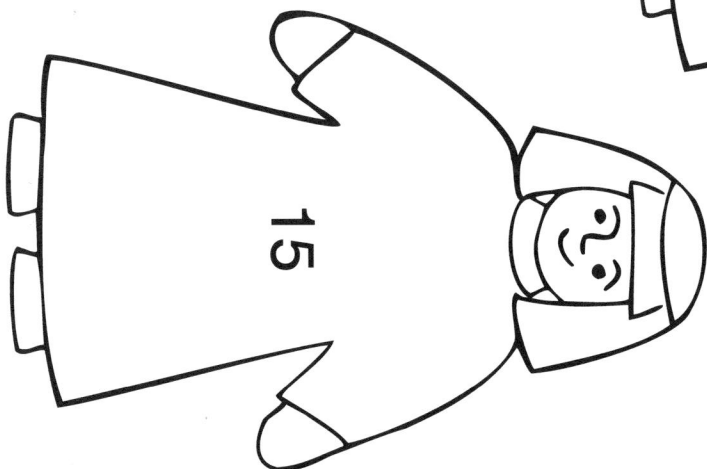

Jesus Helps ...

10 lepers.   Luke 17:11-19

What was the problem?

The men had a skin disease that meant

☐ they could not talk to people

☐ they could not go near people

☐ they could not enter a village

How many men were healed?

☐ 1

☐ 9

☐ 10

How did Jesus heal the men?

☐ with a word

☐ with a touch

Were the men made well   ☐ immediately?

☐ on their way to show the priest?

How many men came back to thank Jesus?

☐ 1

☐ 9

☐ 10

Think of some of the things you can thank God for.

Preparation:
Read John 9:1-41, using the Bible study notes to help you.

Lesson Aim:
To show that spiritual healing is more important than physical healing.

Jesus taught in the previous passage that he is the light of the world (John 8:12). This incident illustrates that fact.

9:1   'Blind from birth' - only the power of Jesus can restore the most extreme cases.

9:2   There was a view at this time that suffering must be caused by someone's sin. The disciples' attitude reflects this.

9:3   Jesus gives an alternative view.

9:4   'The night comes' could mean the close of Jesus' mission.

9:5   Jesus makes his claim before he performs the miracle (see also 8:12 and 1:9). This is another way of Jesus making himself known as the Messiah - he is the true light that shows the true way. He gives spiritual sight as well as physical sight.

9:6-7   His faith produced obedience which led to his healing.

9:16   The Pharisees did not see an act of mercy as justification for breaking the Sabbath.

9:17   They quizzed him persistently to see if he would break and tell a different story. Instead, gradually he begins to realise that Jesus is someone special. He is later to find out just how special!

9:18-22   The authorities were determined to discredit the story. They hoped the parents would assist but found no help there. The parents did not want to be involved. We are told that this was because of fear.

9:24-25   'We know ....' contrasts with the man's 'I know ....'. He had had a personal experience of Jesus.

9:26-27   The man is put out that they ask him to repeat the details of his healing.

9:30-33   The man's reasoning was something as follows:

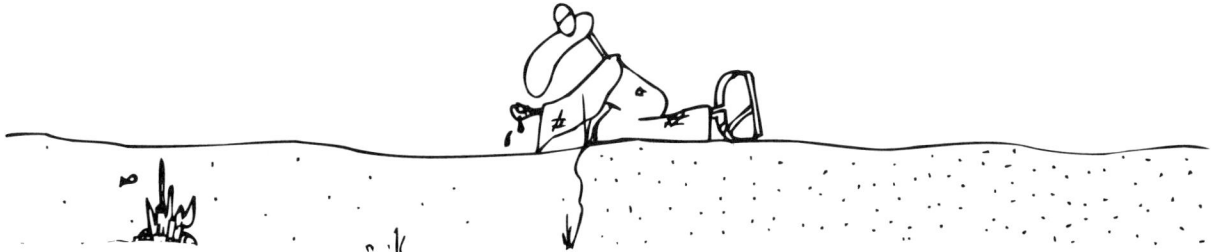

- his sight has been restored.
- God only listens to the prayers of those who are obedient to him.
- therefore, the healing shows Jesus cannot be a sinner.
- to restore the sight of someone born blind is without precedent.
- The healing shows that not only is the healer from God, but he must also be someone special to have been able to do such a unique thing.

9:35   Now we read about the man's personal interview with Jesus, which reaches its climax in his declaration of faith. Jesus takes the initiative to find the man. (He also took the initiative in the original healing.) The sign (miracle) here leads the man to faith.

9:36   He makes a perfectly valid request.

9:37-38   As soon as he recognises that Jesus is the Son of Man he confesses his faith in him as Lord. Faith had already started to grow (see 9:7,31-33). Now we see the climax - 'he worshipped him'. The Jews only worshipped God.

Summary The parents readily accept the evidence of the healing, but are reluctant to openly admit the implication. The Pharisees are eventually forced to accept the evidence of their eyes, but refuse to accept the obvious conclusion. The man gratefully accepts the healing as evidence of who Jesus is and responds in faith. The healing miracle should strengthen our faith and lead us to see the true light. The importance of the story is that the man believed and showed his faith by worshiping Jesus.

Lesson Plan

Talk about children with different needs. A group of children are playing together, but one child is sitting apart and lonely. A group of children all have smart name-brand trainers, but one child only has old, tatty ones. A group of children are playing football, but one child is on the side lines with a leg in plaster. Use other examples as you see fit. Discuss the different needs portrayed in the situations and how those needs can be met. We know about those needs because we can see them. What about the needs we cannot see, those inside us? Who can see those? In today's true story from the Bible we will learn about a man who had outside needs and inside ones. Ask the children to listen carefully so that they can tell you what the man's outside need was, what his inside need was and which was the most important. Tell the story.

After the story go over the answers to the questions and recap on what a miracle is. Ask the older children how this miracle differs from the previous ones studied. Point out to the children that God wants to make us well inside by forgiving our sins.

Visual Aids

Pictures or flannelgraph. You need the blind man, his parents, religious leaders.

Activities / 3 - 5s

Make a story box. Photocopy pages 53 and 64 on card for each child. Prior to the lesson cut out the story box and make up according to the instructions on page 64 Cut out the 4 pictures from pages 53 and 64 and place in an envelope for each child. The children colour the pictures and glue them in order around the box.

Activities / 5 - 7s

Photocopy page 65 for each child. Prior to the lesson cut out the 2 eye sockets on the man's face. Cut off the bottom section of the page and cut out the 2 circles. Attach the 2 circles behind the man's face using split pin paper fasteners at X. Start with the eye sockets blank to demonstrate the man's blindness. Rotate both circles until the matching eyes appear (only one pair of eyes match). Colour the picture and the eyes, making sure that the matching pair are coloured identically.

Activities / 7 - 9s

Complete the activity book. Photocopy pages 66 and 67 for each child and add to the back of the book. The book can be taken home.

Jesus
is the
Son of God.
1 John 4:15

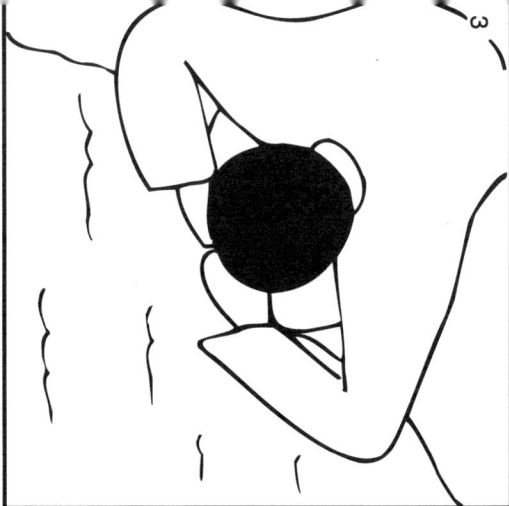

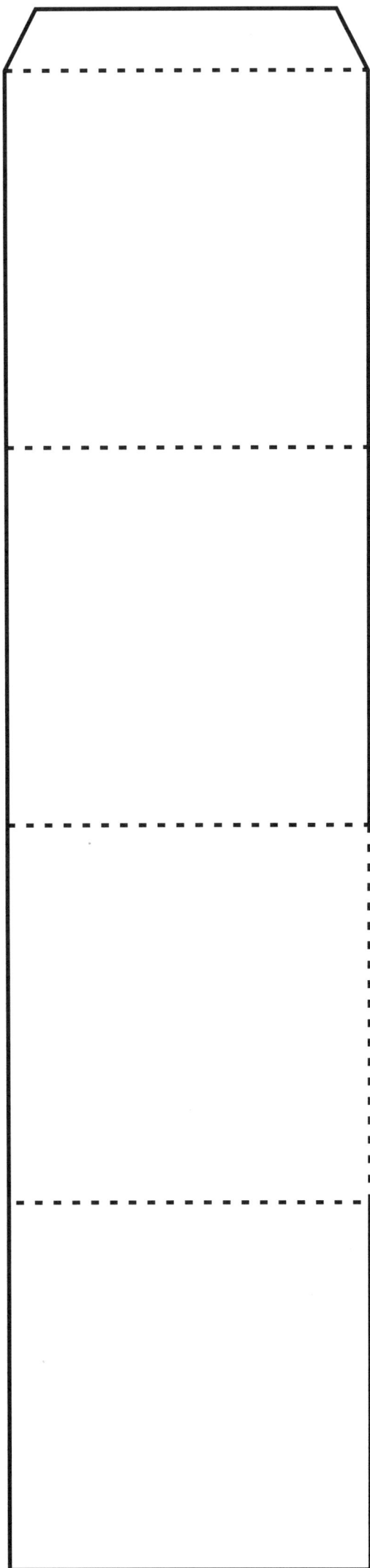

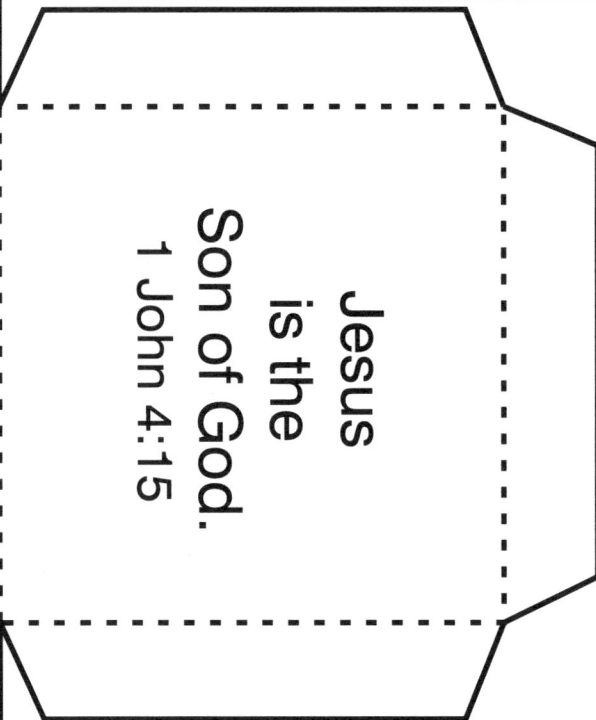

To make up the story box, score and fold along the dotted lines, then glue the tabs in place inside the box.

Jesus is the Son of God.   1 John 4:15

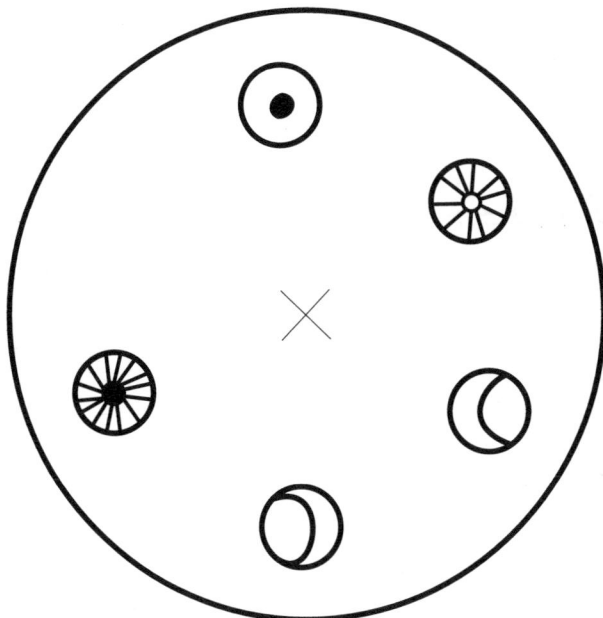

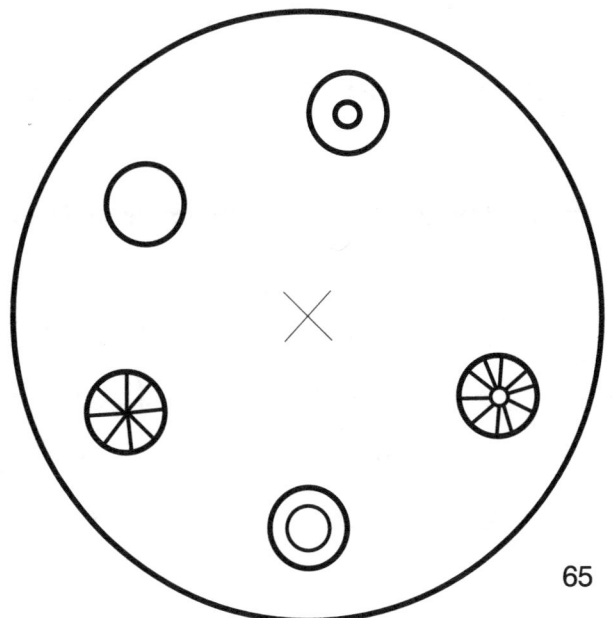

Jesus Helps ...

a blind man.   John 9:1-41

What was the problem?

☐ the man was born blind

☐ the man became blind

Why was the man blind?

☐ he was a sinner

☐ his parents were sinners

☐ to show God's power

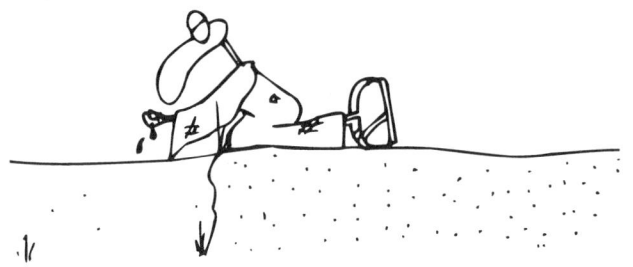

How did Jesus heal the man?

☐ with a word

☐ with a touch

☐ by washing in a pool

What was the result of the miracle?

☐ the man could see

☐ the man believed in Jesus

Which result was the most important?

John 20:31 says the reason for miracles is to bring people to

_ _ _ _ _ in Jesus.

Was this true of the miracles we have studied?

Who believed in Jesus when he helped -

at a wedding (John 2:1-11)?

a sick son (John 4:46-54)?

a crippled woman (Luke 13:10-17)?

10 lepers (Luke 17:11-19)?

a blind man (John 9:1-41)?

Help the blind man find his way to the Pool of Siloam.

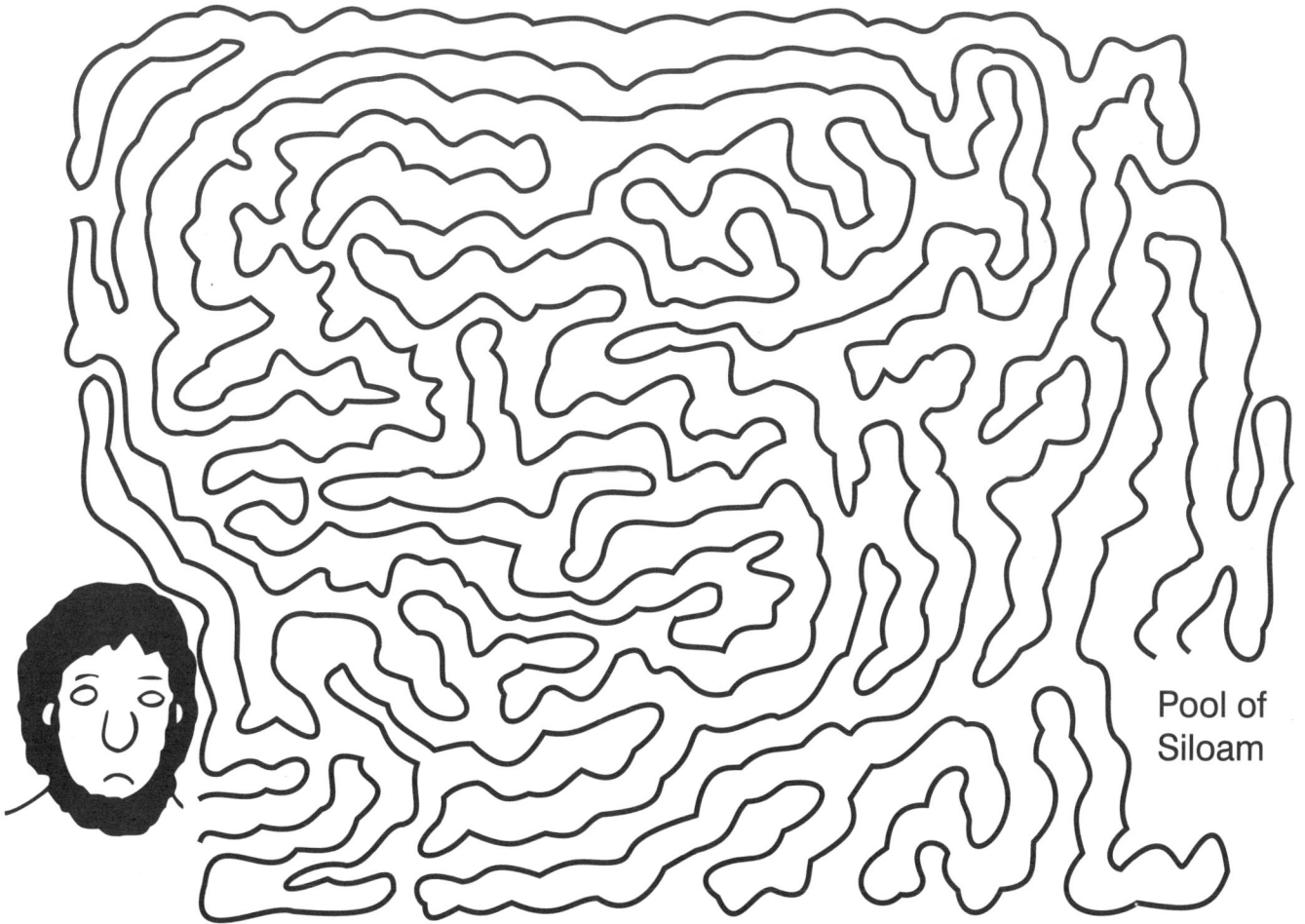

Pool of
Siloam

Colour in the memory verse.

Jesus is the Son of God.
1 John 4:15

Parables of the Kingdom

Overview

Week 11

THE PARABLE OF THE SOWER   *Matthew 13:1-23*

To understand the need to respond to God's word and to put it into practice.

Week 12

THE PARABLE OF THE WEEDS   *Matthew 13:24-30,36-43*

To teach that good and evil co-exist in the world and will do so until Jesus comes again.

Week 13

THE PARABLES OF THE HIDDEN TREASURE AND THE PEARL   *Matthew 13:44-46*

To teach that belonging to God's kingdom is worth any sacrifice.

Week 14

THE PARABLE OF THE GREAT FEAST   *Luke 14:15-24*

To understand that those who reject God's invitation to be part of

Series Aims

1. To understand what a parable is.
2. To understand what it means to be part of God's kingdom.

Jesus often used parables in his teaching (Matthew 13:34-35). A parable is a story or saying designed to teach a spiritual truth, and they are not always as easy to understand as they seem at first. Parables are very similar to allegories - both present interesting illustrations from which can be drawn moral and religious truths. Parables are short, descriptive stories which are usually designed to present a single truth or answer a single question, (e.g. Luke 10:25-37). An allegory differs from a parable in that most of its details have their counterparts in the application, e.g. the parable of the sower. Both forms are found in the gospels.

Parables are the appropriate form of communication for bringing men the message of the kingdom, since their function is to jolt the hearers into seeing things in a new way. They are intended to bring the hearers to a point of decision by using imagery that is familiar, to bring new and unfamiliar insights to them. The parables were meant to force people to decide about their attitude to Jesus and his message.

The Jews were looking forward to the coming of God's kingdom as a time when God would intervene to restore his people's fortunes and save them from their enemies. E.g. in the time of Jesus the Jews were looking for a Messiah to deliver them from the Romans and make them into a great nation, as they were in the time of David and Solomon. John the Baptist preached that this kingdom was at hand (Matthew 3:1-2), but stressed that the king would come as judge as well as saviour. This judgment would be unavoidable, so John called on his hearers to repent and be baptised as the only means of escaping God's anger (Matthew 3:7-12). Jesus proclaimed the coming of this kingdom in the same way as John had (Matthew 4:17, Mark 1:14-15), but stated that the kingdom had now arrived (Matthew 12:28). God's kingdom has come in the person of Jesus, and in this present age (the length of which no-one knows - Mark 13:32) is seen as a reality in the church. It is only when Jesus comes again in glory that his kingdom will be seen in all its fullness. As a result, many of the parables have a present as well as a future application. The parables that relate to God's kingdom teach about its nature, its coming, its value, its growth, and the sacrifices it calls for.

Matthew chapter 13 contains 8 parables about the kingdom. The first 4 were spoken to the crowd - the sower (v.1-23), the weeds (v.24-30,36-43), the mustard seed (v.31-32), and the yeast (v.33) - and the second 4 to the disciples - the hidden treasure (v.44), the pearl (v.45-46), the net (v.47-50), and the house owner (v.52). They come at a point when Jesus has demonstrated his Messiahship yet has been met with unbelief (Matthew chaps. 11-12).

This series looks at the parables of the sower, the weeds and the hidden treasure and the pearl, and also the parable of the great feast (Luke 14:15-24). They look at the reality of Jesus' kingship and the need to respond to his word by becoming part of his kingdom (the sower). The parable of the weeds teaches us not to be discouraged by the presence of evil in our world - it does not mean that God has lost control. The parables of the hidden treasure and the pearl deal with the value of the kingdom, and the parable of the great feast warns about the danger of rejecting God's invitation to be part of his kingdom.

Memory Work

3-5s   Seek first God's kingdom.

Matthew 6:33

5-9s   Seek first God's kingdom and his righteousness.

Matthew 6:33

Visual Aids for the Sower

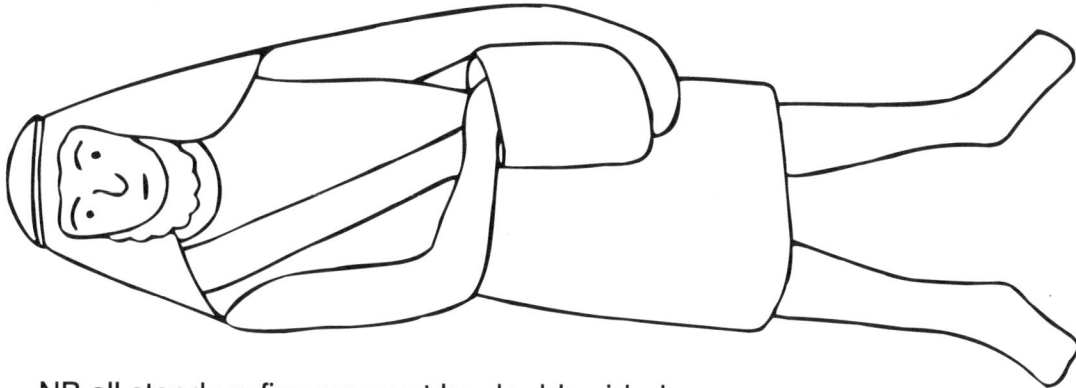

NB all stand up figures must be double sided.

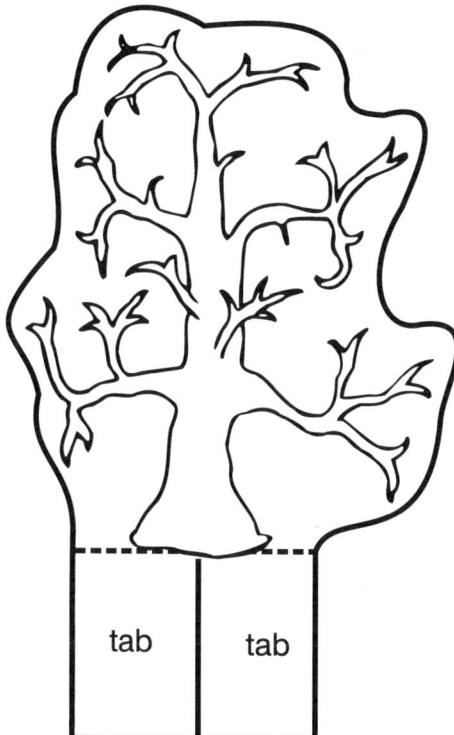

thorn bush (2 required)

For stand up figures, glue onto card, cut out and colour both sides. Fold along dotted line. Cut tab in half where indicated and fold the 2 halves in opposite directions. Glue or blue-tak to base.

tab   tab

Preparation:
Read Matthew 13:1-23, using the Bible study notes to help you.

Lesson Aim:
To understand the need to respond to God's word and to put it into practice.

This parable is also recorded in Mark 4:1-20 and Luke 8:1-15.

This parable (and the others in chapter 13) illustrates and brings home the teaching of the previous chapters. Jesus condemned the towns of Galilee for their failure to respond to his miracles. These were evidence of the presence of the holy son of God in their midst and the natural reaction should have been repentance. The Jewish leaders could not understand that demons could only be driven out by the power of the Holy Spirit (12:28). Why was it that so many failed to understand that the kingdom of heaven had come in the person of Jesus? Amongst the parables of the kingdom, the parable of the sower (so called by Jesus, v.18) is usually seen as the key teaching. This is the first of only 2 parables where Jesus gives the interpretation (v.18-23, v.36-43).

13:1   The day referred to is the one when Jesus healed a demon-possessed man and was accused by the Pharisees of being himself under the power of Beelzebub (Satan), Matthew 12:22-24. Also on that same day Jesus' mother and brothers had come looking for him and Jesus stated that his real mother and brothers were not his natural family but his disciples - those who did the will of his father in heaven (12:46-50).

The parable was spoken to the crowd, but the interpretation was only given to the disciples (vv.10,18).

13:11   The ability to interpret parables is a gift from God and is not dependent on human wisdom.

13:12   What you get out of something depends on what you can put into it. This explains why the same parable meets with different responses.

13:13-15   See Isaiah 6:9-10. Jesus is not saying that he told parables in order to conceal the truth and therefore keep people out of the kingdom, but that parables reveal who has been given the ability to understand them and therefore demonstrate who is a disciple of Jesus.

13:17   The disciples are favoured because they are seeing the reality of the kingdom.

13:18-23   The interpretation.

Parable	Explanation
farmer sows the seed	hearing the message of the kingdom
seed on the path	failure to understand
seed on rocky places	superficial response
seed among thorns	response choked by the cares of the world
seed on good soil	hearing and understanding

13:23   The person who truly understands will also act and produce fruit. See Galatians 5:22-23, James 2:17.

Lesson Plan

Plant some cress with the children. Talk about the conditions that seeds need in order to grow. Show the children a picture of the plant when it is grown (see the seed packet). Ask the children what the cress can be used for. Put the cress aside for next week. In today's true story from the Bible we will hear a story that Jesus told. Explain what a parable is (see page 68). Tell the story.

At the end of the story go over the meaning of the parable and teach the memory verse.

Visual Aids

For a small class that can sit round a table and see what is on it
- A tray or sheet of brown paper.
- A strip of grey paper (the path).
- Soil for either side of the path (optional).
- Small stones (or shapes cut out of grey paper).
- 2 thorn bushes.

This needs to be set up before the lesson (see diagram).

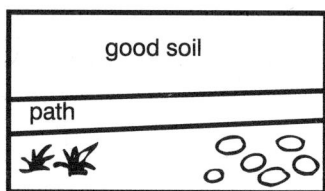

2 thorn bushes   rocky ground

You also need 1 packet of seeds and 1 sower, a bird finger puppet, and strips of corn (see pages 69, 72 and 73).

Position the sower to the left of the tray. Scatter seed from the packet on the 4 areas as you tell the story.

The strip of corn for the rocky ground is folded at the dotted line so that the tab makes a right angle with the strip. When placed on the rocky ground it will stand for a short while before toppling over. (If necessary, a gentle push will ensure that it does!)

The strip of corn for the thorn bushes is attached at either end to cocktail sticks (this will keep it upright). Place a small piece of blue-tak on the bottom of each stick. When these are stuck onto the tray the strip will stand up.

The strip of thorns choking the corn is folded in half and joined at the ends to make a double strip (picture on outside) that can be slotted over the corn growing among the thorns.

The strip of corn growing in good ground is set up with cocktail sticks and blue-tak in the same way as the corn growing among the thorns.

NB All figures must have the picture on both sides.

For a larger class

A large sheet of paper pinned to a board on which is a path, some thorn bushes, rocky ground, good soil, sky and sun (see diagram).

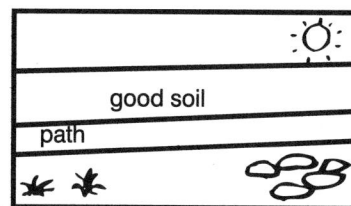

2 thorn bushes   rocky ground

You also need a sower, cut-outs of seed, birds and strips of corn from pages 69, 72 and 73.

Position the sower to the left hand side of the background. Place seed cut-outs onto the 4 areas as you tell the story. This can be done using bluetak. Add the other visuals as the story progresses.

Having told the story, discuss the meaning of each type of soil with the children. See if they can work out what the thorns are, (e.g. sport, friends, hobbies), and the rocky ground - being laughed at for being a Christian (v.21).

Activities / 3 - 5s

Photocopy pages 74 and 75 for each child. Prior to the lesson cut around the solid lines on page 75 and fold the windows open along the dotted lines. Glue page 74 behind page 75, gluing at the edges only so that the windows can be opened to see what is behind them. Colour the pictures and either glue rice grains onto the pictures on the top page or draw seed. Open the windows to see what happened to each lot of seed.

Activities / 5 - 7s

Photocopy pages 76 and 77 for each child. Prior to the lesson cut slits in the hatched areas on page 77 and cut out the long strips from page 76. Colour the strips and insert them into page 77 (see diagram), so that they can be pulled backwards and forwards to reveal the parable's meaning.

Activities / 7 - 9s

Photocopy pages 78 and 79 back to back for each child. Cut out the cross shape and fold along the dotted lines. Fold together by folding in no.8 first, then no.5, then no.3 and lastly no.2. 'The Parable of the Sower' should now be uppermost.

Go through the parable as a group activity and fill in the missing words. The story unfolds bit by bit and the meaning only becomes clear as more pages unfold. Point out to the children that this is the same for a parable - we need to delve deeper if we want to understand the meaning.

Other activities

Acting out the story. The characters required are the sower, bird(s), seed on rocky ground (grows up then falls over), seed among thorns, thorn bush(es), seed on good ground. The teacher tells the story and the children act it out. The seeds can have great fun growing up and wilting or being choked by the thorn bush. The seed on good ground should be the only one(s) left standing at the end. **NB** do keep an eye on the choking - it does not need to be too enthusiastic!

Planting seed. This can either be a joint class activity and the pot left at Sunday School for checking the following week, or each child can plant a small pot and take it home.

Requirements: 1 packet of cress seeds, 1 container with soil, 1 container with blotting paper and 1 empty container.

Instructions: plant seeds in each container and water. Empty the water out of the empty container so that the seeds are not left sitting in a pool of water. The seeds in the soil should grow, those on the blotting paper should start to sprout but when the blotting paper dries they will fall over.

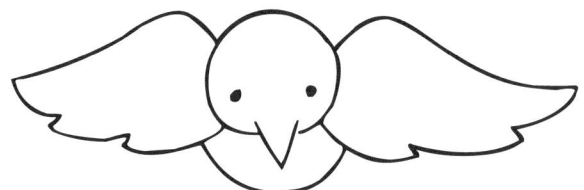

Visual Aids

seed

bird finger puppet
(glue onto card)

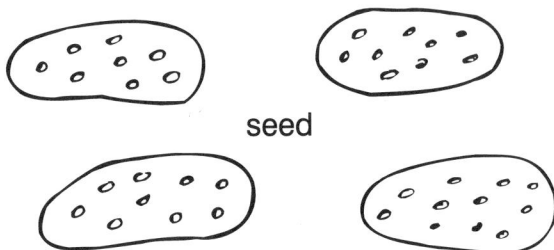

strip to glue into a ring
and attach to back of bird

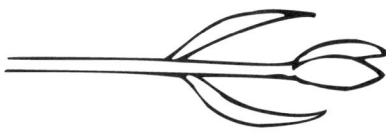

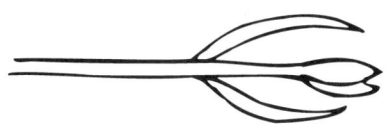

amongst thorns

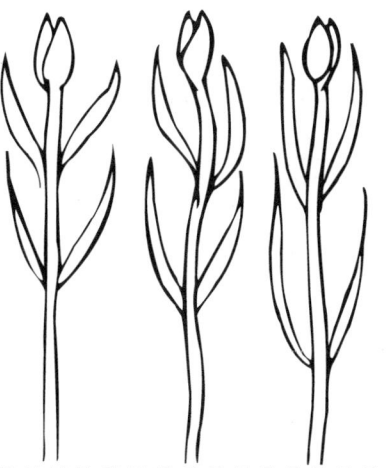

tab (rocky ground)

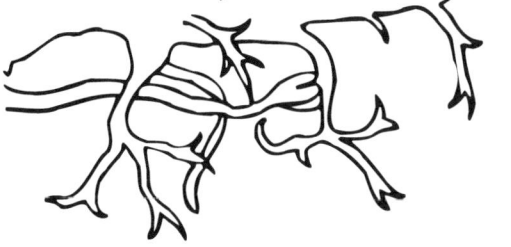

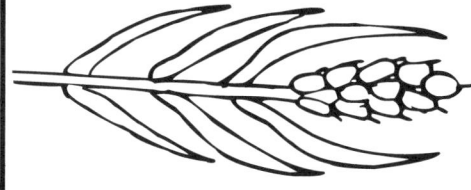

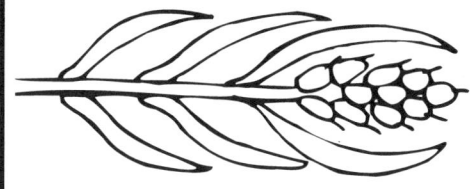

good ground

Birds ate the seed.

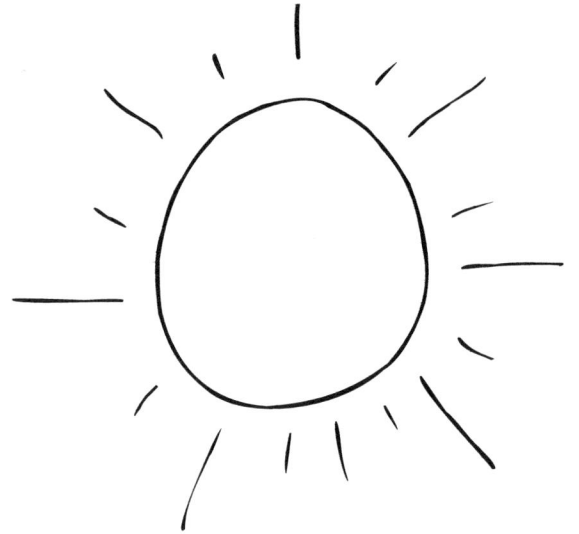

The sun burnt the shoots.

Thorns choked the plants.

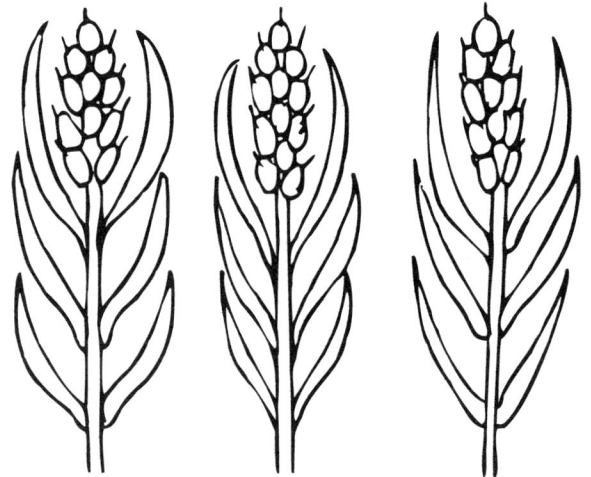

The good soil grew
lots of strong plants.

Listen to God's Word.

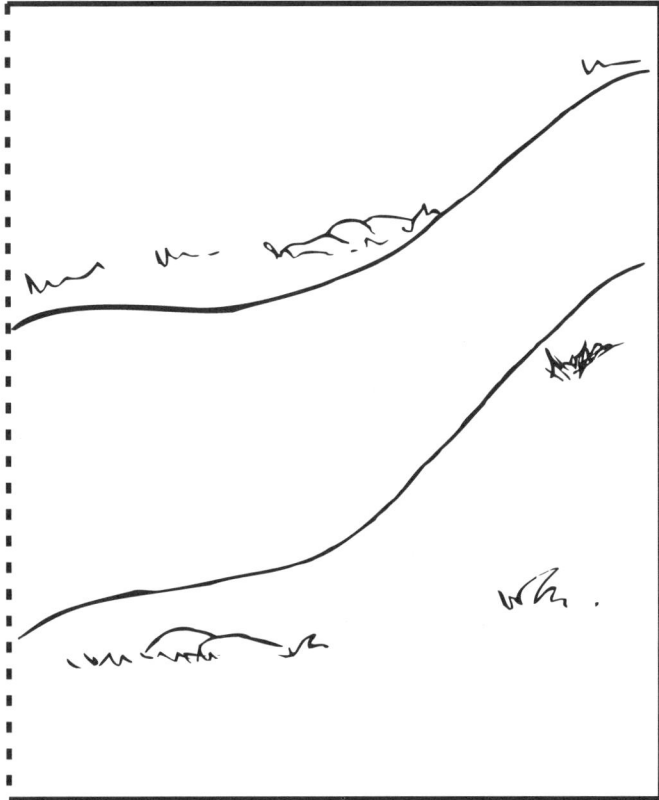

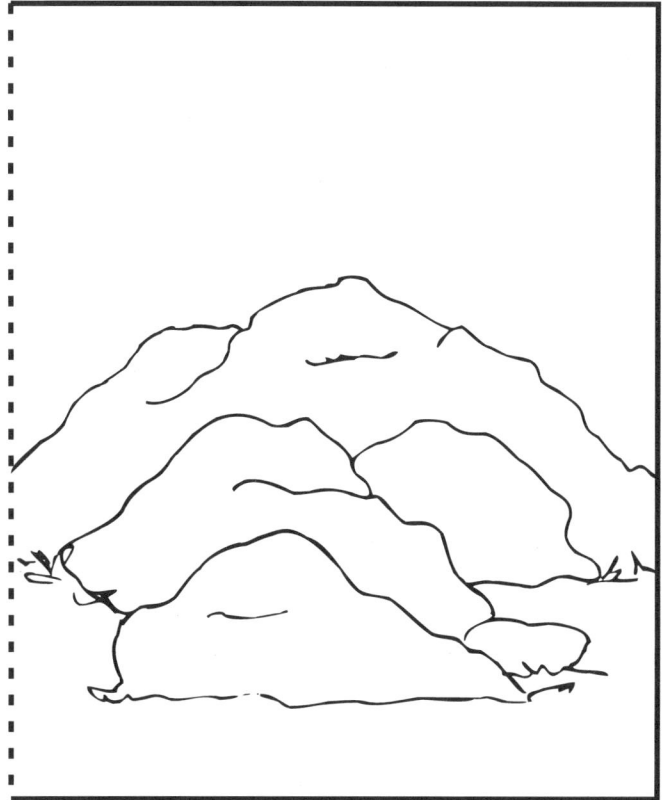

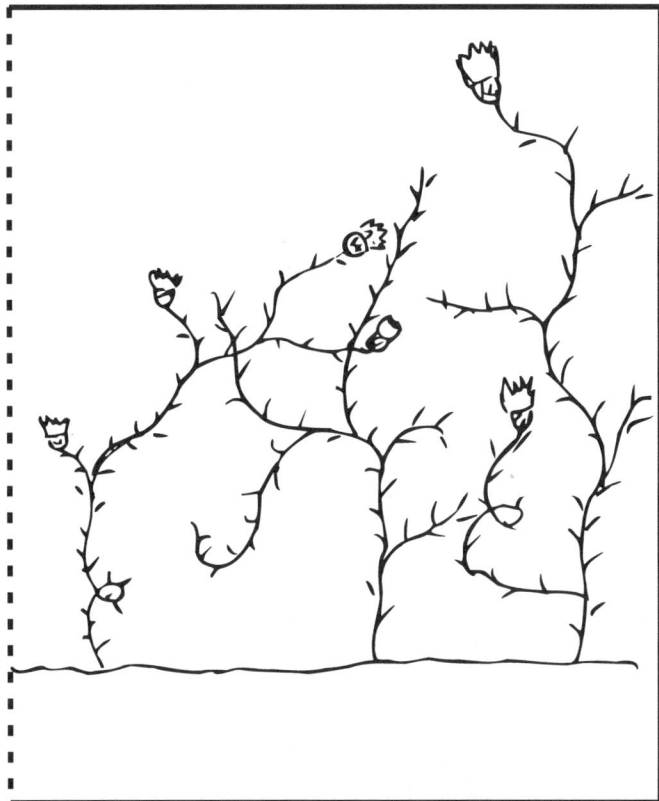

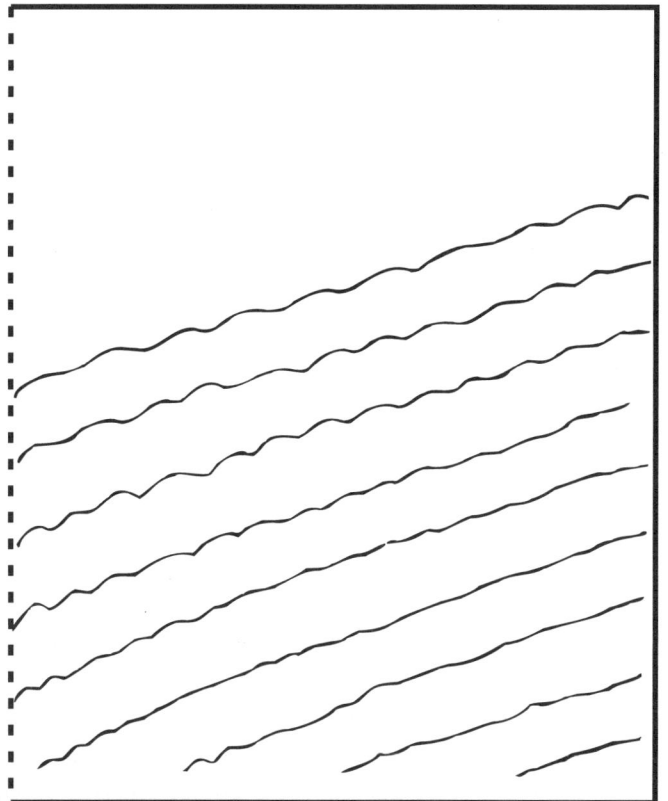

Do what God says. Matthew 13:1-23

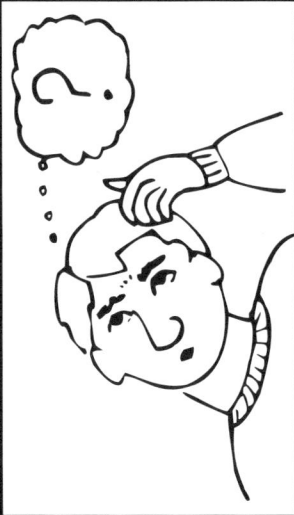

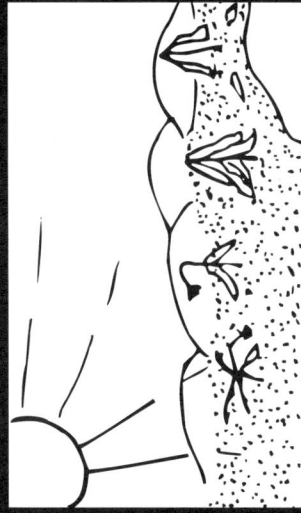

The Parable of the Sower

Matthew 13:1-23

Seek first God's kingdom and his righteousness.

Matthew 6:33

3. Some fell among
t _ _ _ _ _ , which grew
up and c _ _ _ _ _ the
plants (v.7).

5. The seeds that fall
along the p _ _ _
are those who h _ _ _
God's word but do
_ _ _ understand
it (v.19).

7. The thorn bushes are
those who h _ _ _
God's word, but
w _ _ _ _ _ _ about
this life and l _ _ _
for riches choke the
message (v.22).

8. The g _ _ _ ground
is those who h _ _ _
God's word and
u _ _ _ _ _ _ _ _ _ _ it.
They grow up and
bear f _ _ _ _ (v.23).
(Now turn over.)

2. Some fell on r _ _ _ _
ground. When the
_ _ _ came up the
plants withered and
d _ _ _ (v.5-6).

1. Some seed fell along
the _ _ _ _ and the
_ _ _ _ _ came and
ate it up (v.4).

6. The r _ _ _ _ ground
is those who hear
God's word g _ _ _ _ _ _,
but when trouble
comes they give _ _
at once (v.20-21).

Which

ground

are you?

4. Some fell on _ _ _ _
ground and the plants
produced c _ _ _ (v.8.)

Jesus said: Once
there was a man who
went to sow corn,

Matthew 13:1-23
the Sower
The Parable of

Preparation:
Read Matthew 13:24-30, 36-43, using the Bible study notes to help you.

Lesson Aim:
To teach that good and evil co-exist in the world and will do so until Jesus comes again

This parable is unique to Matthew's gospel.

13:25   It has been suggested that the weeds were 'bearded Darnel', a poisonous rye-grass common in the East. It looked very like wheat until the head appeared. According to ancient Jewish ideas the weeds were not from different seed but only a degenerate kind of wheat. The Jewish hearers would therefore think of these weeds as degenerate kinds of wheat, wholly indistinguishable from the wheat until the fruit appeared.

13:29   Note the gracious concern of God that not one believer should be lost.

13:30   Just as, therefore, we are to expect the continuation of sin and evil in the world throughout the present age (see also

Matthew 24:6 ff.), so also there is bound to be a mixed community within the church. This is evident throughout the letters of Paul and Peter, (e.g. 2 Peter 2:1-3). Therefore, we must not become discouraged.

13:36-43   The interpretation of the parable.

Lesson Plan

Use the cress planted last week to demonstrate what happens if you try and pull up a seedling. You cannot remove one without disturbing the rest. Ask the children if they would risk damaging a precious one by removing the other ones round it. Show the children a jar of brown sugar and salt mixed together. How can you separate the sugar from the salt without ruining it? In today's true story from the Bible we will hear a story Jesus told about 2 things that were mixed up and needed separating. Remind the

children what a parable is. Ask the children to listen carefully so that they can tell you what the 2 things were and how they were separated. Tell the story.

At the end of the story go over the answers to the questions and revise the memory verse. Point out to the children how precious God's people are to him.

Visual Aids

A large sheet of paper to act as a background.
A piece of black paper to cover the sky, with moon and stars on it.
A sower.
An enemy.
1 green pen, 1 yellow pen, 1 brown pen.

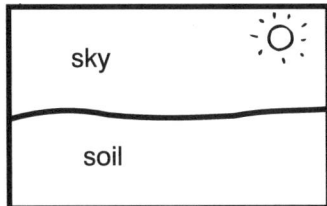

Fix the sower onto the background when the seed is being sown. Remove the sower and place night sky in place. Fix the enemy onto the background to sow the seed. Remove the night sky. Use the green pen to make small lines over the soil to demonstrate seed sprouting (see diagram).

Lengthen the lines and add leaves. Use the yellow pen to draw in the corn on top of some shoots. Use the brown pen to draw in tops on weeds (see diagram).

This parable can be acted out very effectively as a means of recapping the story.

Activities / 3 - 5s

Photocopy page 82 for each child. Ask the children if they can pick out which plants are weeds and which wheat? Colour the picture according to the code at the top. It is only when the heads are coloured that the difference can be seen.

Activities / 5 - 7s

Photocopy pages 83 and 84 back to back for each child.

Prior to the lesson, prepare an enlarged form of the word square for the board. Ask the children to call out any words they can find. As each word is identified outline it on the word square on the board and ask the children to outline it on their own puzzle sheet.

The tracing of wheat and weeds can be done by the children.

Break the code - do this as a joint activity. Ask the children to call out the symbols one at a time, making sure that **all** the children are included. Write the first letter of each symbol on the board and ask the children to do the same on their puzzle sheets.

Activities / 7 - 9s

Photocopy pages 85 and 86 back to back for each child. Having completed the puzzles discuss the good and bad categories. Talk through bullying, etc. If a child is being bullied does this mean that God does not care? Is it because the child has been naughty and God is punishing him/her? The above 2 questions are common misapprehensions and need to be brought out into the open so that they can be dealt with.

Craft
✓ A3 paper
✓ black paper
    moon & stars
        ↳ card, silver foil,
    brown paper stars
    a sower
    an enemy
    felt pens
    blue tack
    fello.
    wheat & weeds

Can you spot the wheat?

Colour the picture to find it.

- ● dark green
- ★ brown
- × light green
- ○ blue
- ☐ yellow

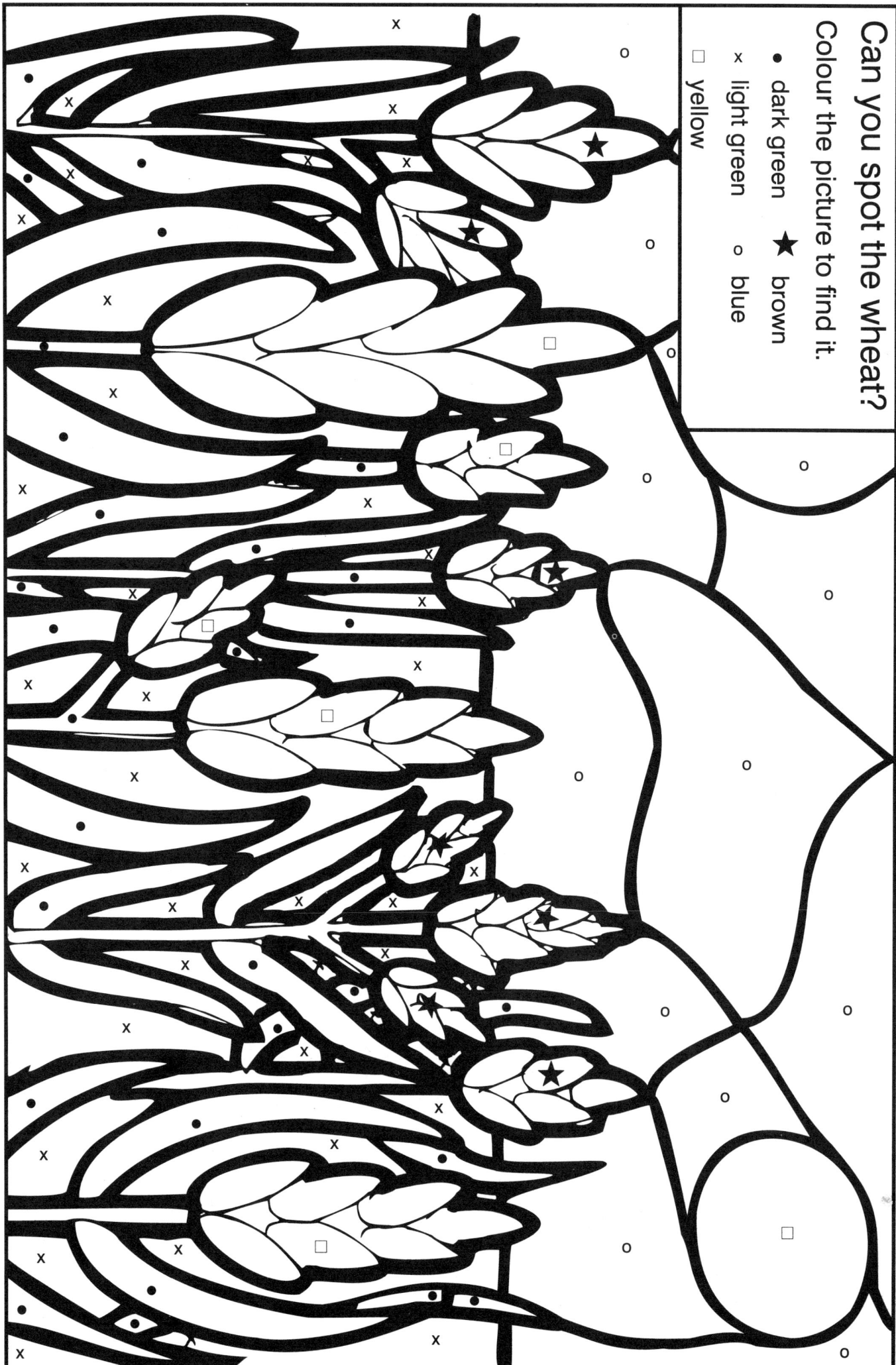

Seek first God's kingdom.   Matthew 6:33

82

How many of these words can you find in the word square?
Some are written across the grid and some down. All are written forwards.

n	h	a	r	v	e	s	t	r	a	r
s	e	e	n	e	m	y	p	o	n	w
o	v	l	t	n	z	i	u	o	g	e
n	i	q	n	w	h	e	a	t	e	e
o	l	t	r	s	o	y	m	r	l	d
f	g	o	o	d	s	e	e	d	s	s
m	e	k	i	n	g	d	o	m	a	s
a	j	f	i	r	e	j	a	s	o	i
n	b	u	r	n	e	d	d	v	w	n

angels
burned
enemy
evil
fire
good seed
harvest
kingdom
root
sin
son of man
weeds
wheat

Which
plants
are
wheat
and
which
are
weeds?

Break the code by writing the first letter of the object in the picture underneath.

God's people will [sun | hat | ice cream | nose | egg] [leg | iron | kite | eye]

_ _ _ _ _   _ _ _ _

[tap | hand | eye] [sheep | umbrella | nib] [ice cream | neck] [bear | house | ear | iron | rabbit]

_ _ _   _ _ _   _ _   _ _ _ _ _

[flower | apple | toe | horse | ear | rainbow | star] [kite | ice cream | nose | giraffe | dog | orange | mouth]

_ _ _ _ _ _ _   _ _ _ _ _ _ _

Matthew 13 v.43

Use the code to discover the memory verse.

Matthew 6:33

Go through the word square, reading from left to right, and colour the letters of the memory verse in the order they come in the verse. If you do this correctly you will have 9 words left in the grid.

	s	e	f	a	i	t	h	e	k
k	i	n	d	n	e	s	s	f	i
r	s	t	G	b	u	l	l	y	o
d	s	h	e	l	p	i	n	g	k
i	n	g	d	o	m	a	n	d	h
i	u	n	b	e	l	i	e	f	s
r	i	g	h	t	l	y	i	n	g
e	s	w	e	a	r	i	n	g	o
u	s	n	e	g	r	e	e	d	s
o	b	e	d	i	e	n	c	e	s

Now sort the remaining words into 2 groups.

good   **bad**

The Parables of the Hidden Treasure and the Pearl

Preparation:
Read Matthew 13:44-46, using the Bible study notes to help you.

Lesson Aim:
To teach that belonging to God's kingdom is worth any sacrifice.

Lesson Plan

These parables are unique to Matthew.

The difference between the two men appears to be that the first man happens to find the treasure, while the second man has been actively searching for fine pearls.

Likewise, some people seem to stumble on the kingdom without apparently being seekers, but God in his grace shows them the truth, while others are actively looking for the truth and may try substitutes. In both cases they are willing to part with everything they have for the great prize they have found. No sacrifice is too big. See Luke 18:18-24.

The children need to understand that to follow Christ and be part of his kingdom means being prepared to give up anything that gets in the way of following God. Try to get them to talk about what they may have to give up and what is the treasure we receive. Stress the benefits of belonging to God's family - but still be realistic about the cost.

Prior to the lesson hide a 'treasure', e.g. a pearl button in the class area. At the start of the lesson tell the children about the treasure and send them off to find it. When they find it they are to come and tell you, leaving the treasure in its hiding place for the rest to find. Alternatively, if you have a large space make a treasure map and send the children off as a group to find the treasure. They can either bring it back or you can have the lesson where it is.

Visual Aids

The teacher acts out the parables as he/she tells them, then get the children to act them out.

Requirements:
- a treasure chest to 'trip over' as you walk across the field
- a bag of money
- pictures of house, car, etc. to 'sell'
- some small 'pearls' plus a big 'pearl' to find as you go from shop to shop.

Activities / 3 - 5s

Each child requires 2 sheets of A4 paper and pages 89 and 90 photocopied on paper. Prior to the lesson cut out the 4 pictures and place in an envelope for each child. Fold the 2 sheets of plain paper in half to make a booklet and staple at the centre. Write the following:

front page   The Parable of the Hidden Treasure
                  Matthew 13:44
back page   Seek first God's kingdom.
                  Matthew 6:33
page 2   A man found some treasure in a field.
page 3   He sold everything that he had.
page 4   With the money he bought the field.
page 5   The man was very, very happy.

The children glue the pictures into the booklet and colour them.

Activities / 5 - 7s

Each child requires an A4 sheet of paper and page 91 photocopied on paper. Prior to the lesson, with the sheet of plain paper landscape, cut a 10 cm. slit about halfway down the right hand side. Write the memory verse along the bottom. Cut out the rectangle, the treasure chest and the man from page 91 and place in an envelope for each child.

Instructions
- Fold the rectangle along the dotted lines and make a pocket behind the slit by gluing the reverse side of X underneath the slit and Z above it (see diagram).
- Glue the man to the left of the slit (see diagram). Draw on details and colour.
- Fold the treasure chest along the dotted line so that the lid can be closed. Draw treasure in the chest and draw in detail on the top of the closed lid.
- Insert the treasure chest into the pocket so that the man can 'find' it.

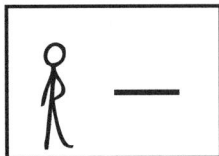

Activities / 7 - 9s

Photocopy page 92 on coloured card, page 93 on white paper and page 94 on coloured paper for each child. Cut out the centre sack shape from page 92, leaving the frame intact. Cut up the solid vertical lines on page 93 as far as the stop line. Sellotape the strips together below the dotted line (see diagram). Cut page 94 into strips as indicated. Discard the top and bottom strip. Weave the coloured strips into page 93 in order to complete the memory verse correctly. Glue the card frame (page 92) on top of the woven mat to secure the edges. The memory verse should be visible in the money sack.

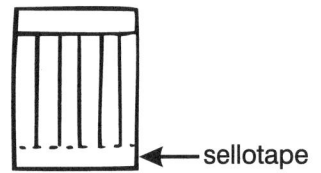

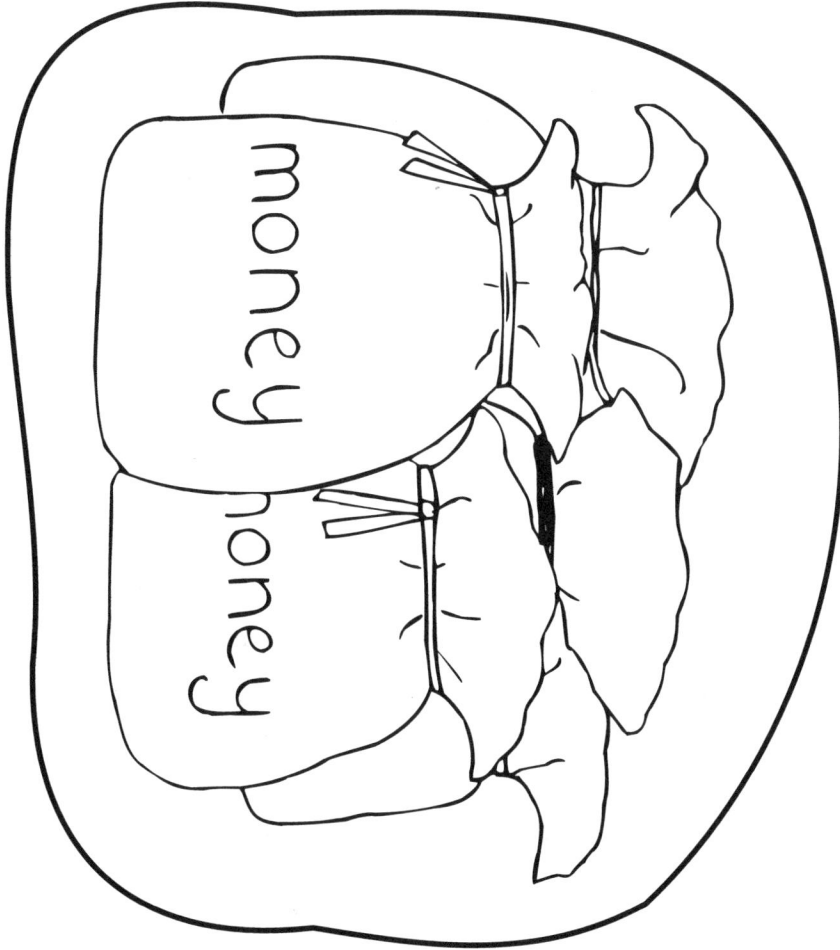

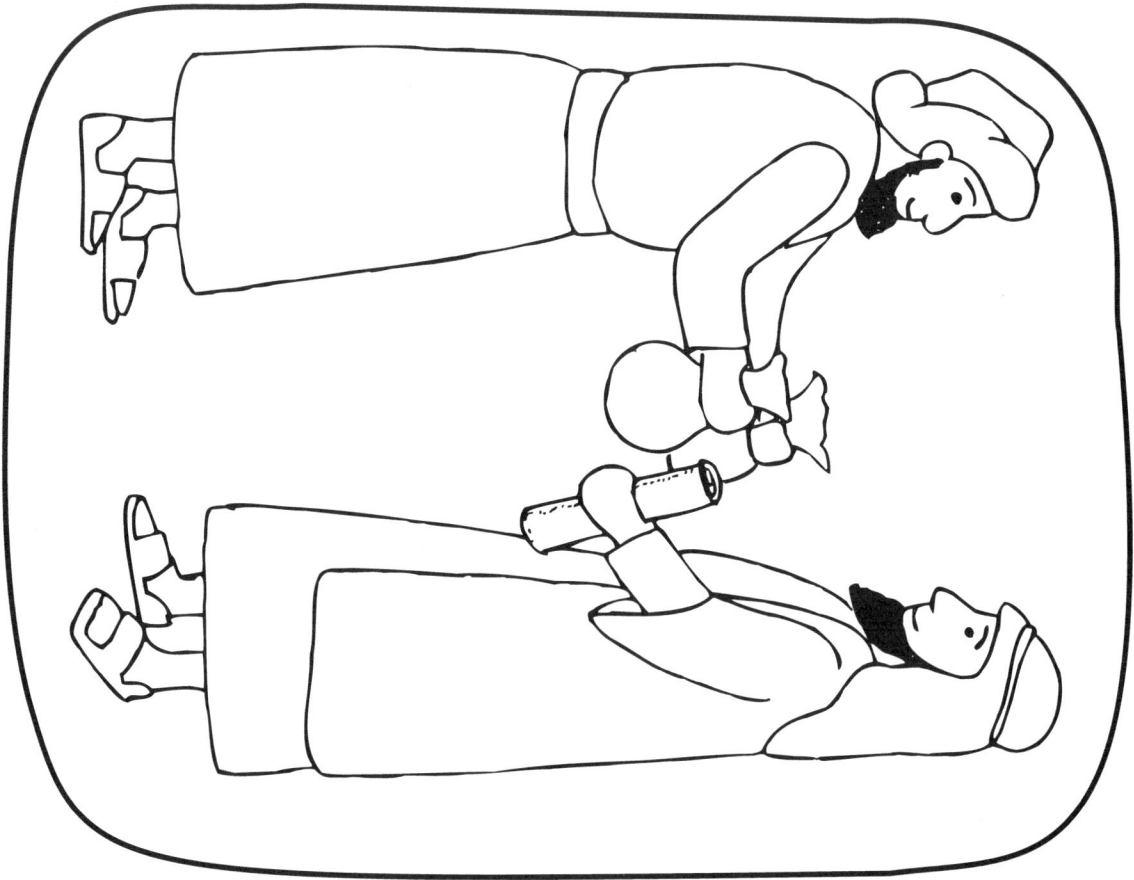

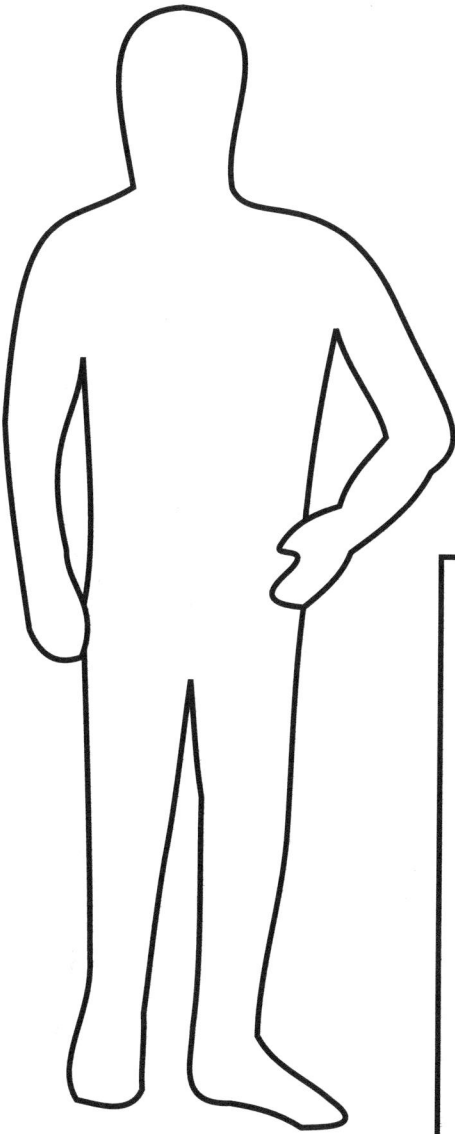

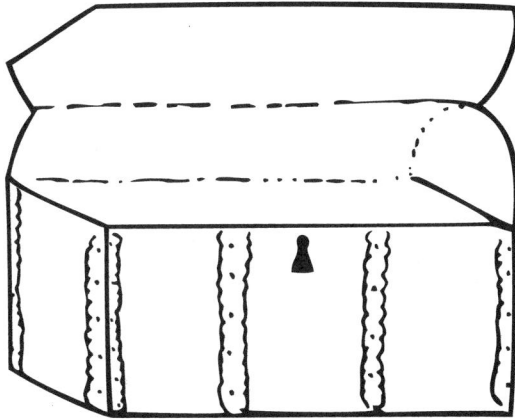

a

b

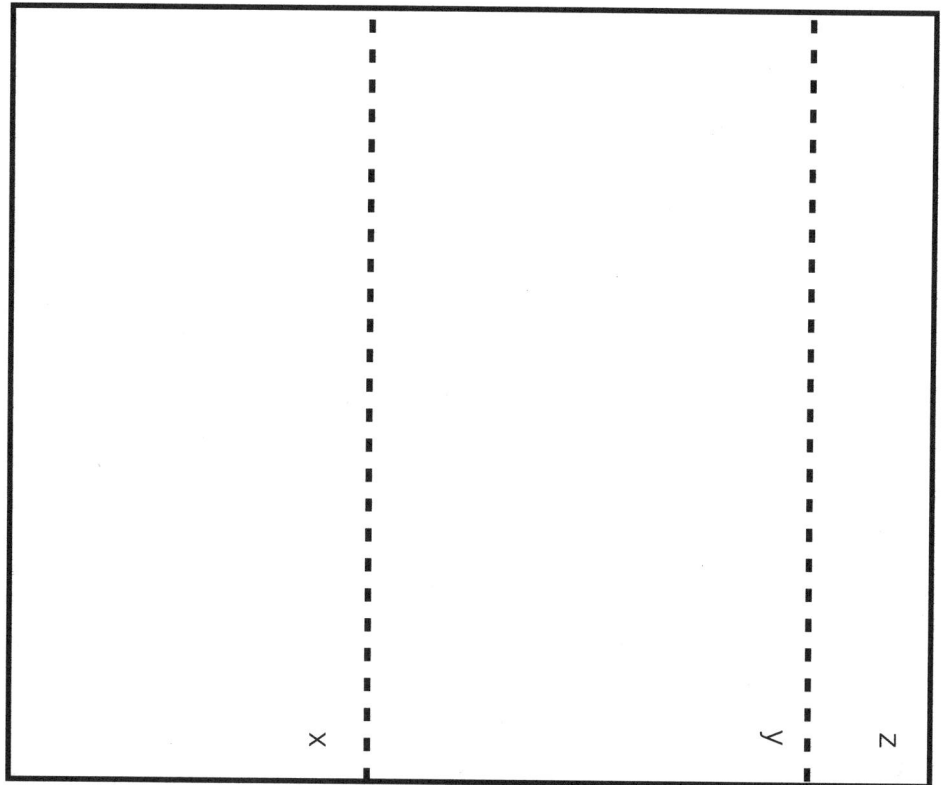

x

y

z

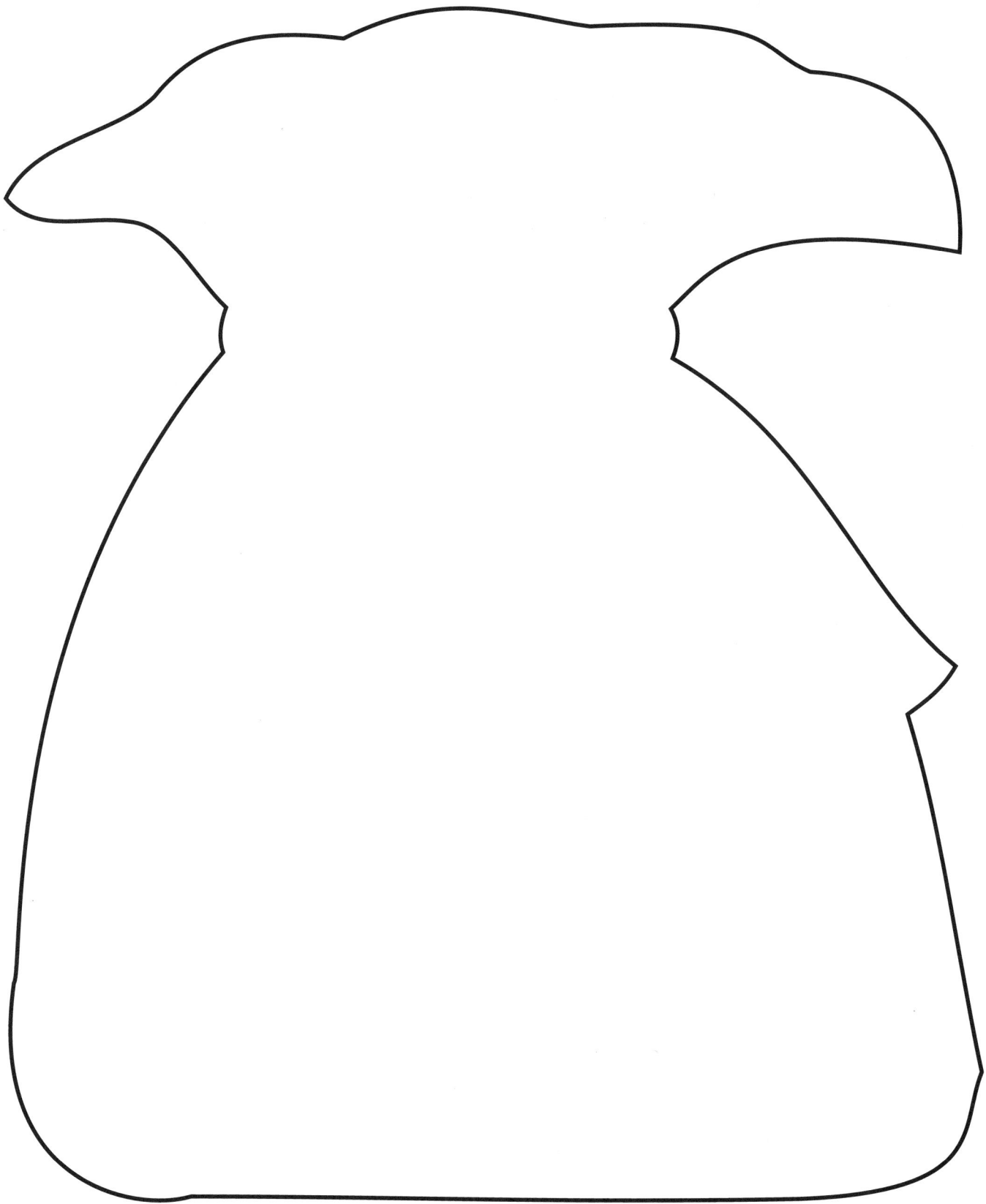

Se

st

Go

do

ki

d

s

ht

us

ss

att

w

33

cut cut cut cut cut cut cut

discard this strip

ek

fir

d's

ng m

an hi

rig eo ne

M he 6:

discard this strip

The Parable of the Great Feast

Preparation:
Read Luke 14:15-24, using the Bible study notes to help you.

Lesson Aim:
To understand that those who reject God's invitation to be part of his kingdom will at the end be rejected by God.

14:15   After Jesus refers to the resurrection (v.14) a guest makes a spontaneous religious exclamation, perhaps a standard formula. It would appear that he believed he would be at the banquet. Jesus challenges this view - would he really be prepared to accept God's invitation?

14:16-17   The practice of an original invitation followed by a reminder was known in the Old Testament (Esther 5:8; 6:14) and later Jewish writings, in which we read 'none of them would attend a banquet unless invited twice'.

14:18   The first man did not want to come. He was using the field as an excuse. Normally a field would be inspected before being bought. Even if this had not

happened it could have waited until after the banquet.

14:19   This excuse was the same as that of the first man.

14:20   This man could have been referring to Deuteronomy 24:5 - but this provision was to free a man from military service in his first year of marriage, not to cut him off from social contact, especially when it had been pre-arranged. His refusal also shows his lack of desire to attend the banquet.

14:21   The master was determined to have the party and so he invited the poor, blind, lame, etc. from the city. (See v.13.)

14:22-23   There was still room, so the servant went to the major roads and the hedges that ran alongside them where very poor, homeless people found shelter. The servant would need to search diligently to find people - but the master means business so the servant must bring them in. There is no idea of forcing people to

come - rather, the servant is to work hard to convince the people that they are wanted.

Here we see a reference to the mission of the church. God had already spoken to the people through the Law and the Prophets. This was rejected, especially by the religious leaders. Now others were being invited - first the despised Jews such as the tax collectors and sinners (the town), then the Gentiles (outside the town). We are not told that this was finished - it is a continuing task.

14:24   Anyone who rejects the Master's invitation will not enjoy the party - God invites us to join him. If we choose not to we will not enter heaven.

This parable demands a response from the children - will they be at God's party in heaven? For any child who is not sure, the teacher needs to be able to present a simple Gospel outline. Page 103 can be coloured and used as a visual aid for this purpose.

Lesson Plan

Talk about getting ready for a party. Ask the children what sort of things you need to do. Send out invitations, set the table, etc. in front of the children. Ask how they would feel if everyone refused to come to their party. Today we will hear another story Jesus told about a man who was giving a party. Ask the children to listen carefully so that they can tell you what excuses people gave for not coming. Remind the children what a parable is. Tell the story.

After the story go over the answers to the question and revise the memory verse. Use the gospel outline on page 103 if required.

Visual Aids

Set up a table ready for a party. Give out an invitation card to half the children in the class. When the party is ready ask each child with an invitation card to come to the party - ask them to shake their head and say 'No'. (The teacher makes the excuses.) Then issue an invitation to the remaining children and persuade them to come to the party.

Activities / 3 - 5s

Make a party headband. Photocopy page 97 on card for each child. Prior to the lesson cut out the 2 pieces and staple or sellotape together at one end. The children decorate their headbands with gummed paper shapes. If time allows have a party.

Activities / 5 - 7s

Photocopy pages 98 and 99 back to back and page 100 single-sided for each child. Cut out the pictures from page 100 and glue onto the spaces in the comic to complete the story. Fill in the missing words and '5' next to 'X' on the oxen picture. The notice on the door in the last picture says 'house full'.

Activities / 7 - 9s

Photocopy page 101 on coloured paper for each child and page 102 on card for every 6 children. Prior to the lesson cut out an invitation card for each child. The children cut out the envelope from page 101 and fold in both side flaps (see diagram). Fold up the bottom flap and glue to the side flaps (see diagram). Fold down the top flap. Write own name on the envelope, then tick the appropriate response on the invitation card and write the memory verse on the back. Decorate the card and envelope if time allows and place the card in the envelope.

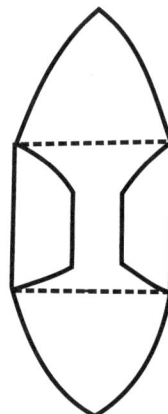

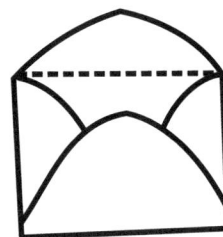

Jesus is the Son of God.   1 John 4:15

On the way to heaven!

The Story of the Great Feast

Luke 14:15-24

A man invited many people to a party.

When the party was ready he sent his servant to tell all the guests to come.

All the guests made excuses. 'I have bought a field and must look at it.'

'I have bought 5 pairs of oxen and must try them out,' said another guest.

A third guest said, 'I can't come because I have just got married.'

The servant told all this to his master. The master was very angry.

He sent his servant to bring in all the poor, crippled, blind and lame people in the town.

But there was still room for more people.

So the servant was sent to the country roads to find more people to come to the party.

h _ _ _ _

f _ _ _

The man said, 'None of those people who refused to come will taste my dinner.'

Seek _ _ _ _ _ _

_ _ _ _ kingdom

and _ _ _

righteousness.

Matthew 6:33

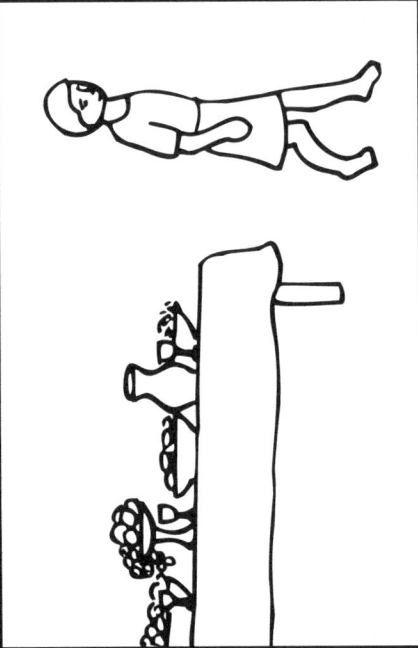

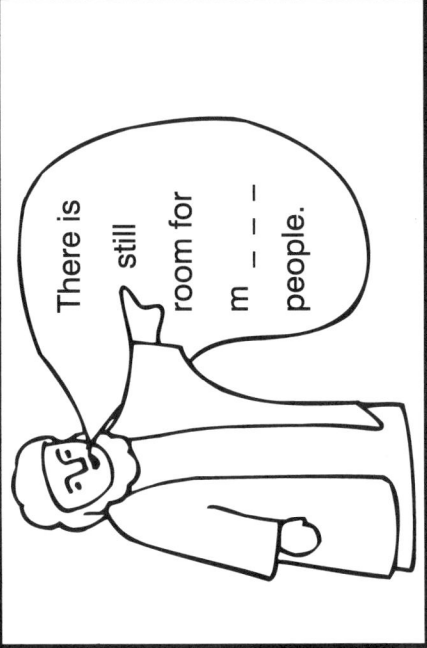

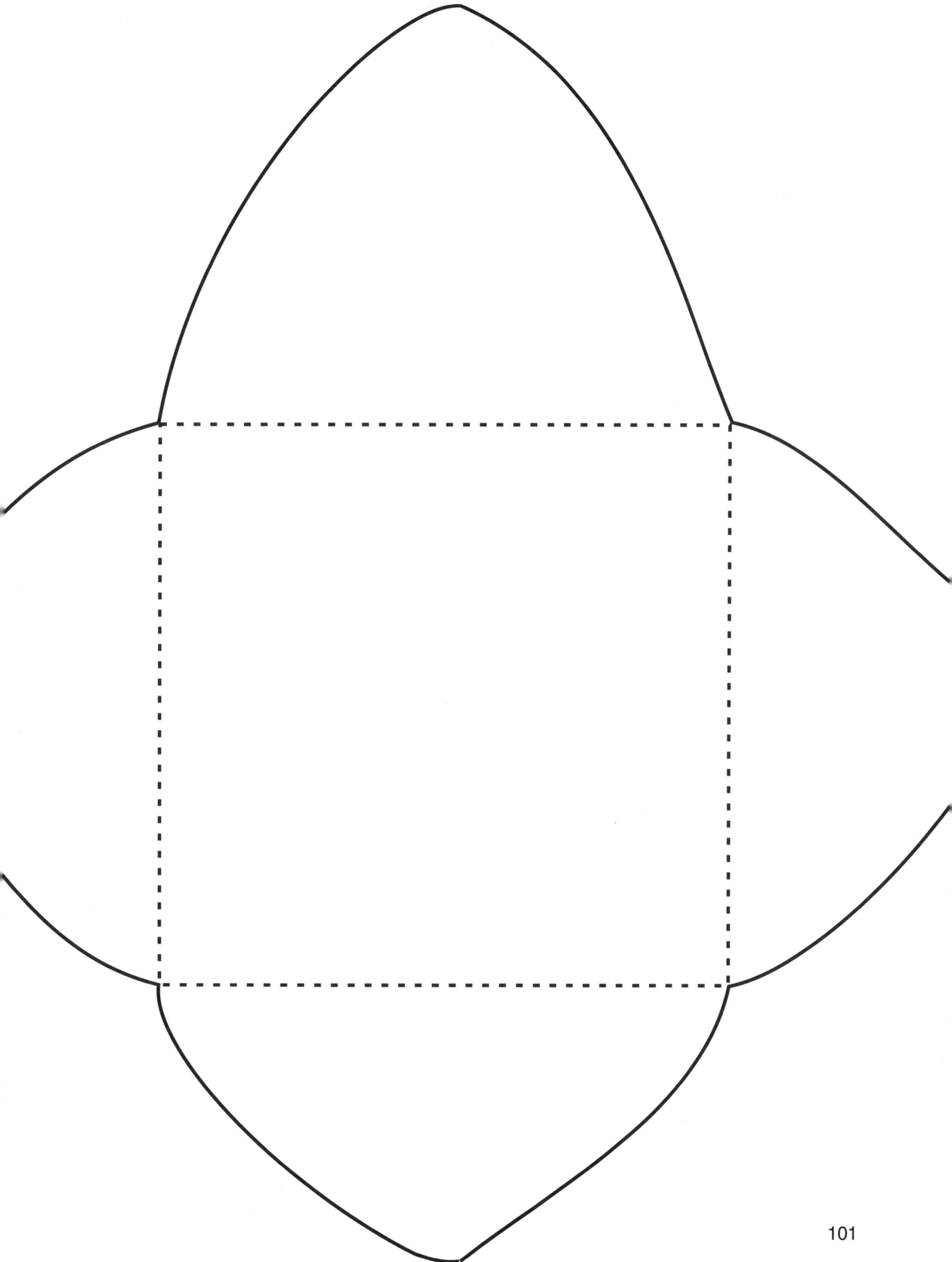

God
invites you to
a party
in heaven
☐ I can come

☐ I cannot come

God
invites you to
a party
in heaven
☐ I can come

☐ I cannot come

God
invites you to
a party
in heaven
☐ I can come

☐ I cannot come

God
invites you to
a party
in heaven
☐ I can come

☐ I cannot come

God
invites you to
a party
in heaven
☐ I can come

☐ I cannot come

God
invites you to
a party
in heaven
☐ I can come

☐ I cannot come

102

God's Good News

God made all things - even me.
Genesis 1:1,31

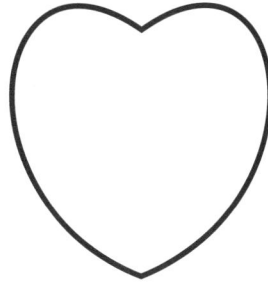

God loves me and wants me to be his friend.
John 3:16

But the wrong things I do put a barrier between me and God.
Isaiah 59:2

To take this barrier away, Jesus died on the cross.
Romans 5:8

Jesus rose from the dead to bring new life to all who believe in him.
Romans 4:25-5:1, 6:23

Sorry, God

If I want to be God's friend I must say sorry to God ******
Acts 2:38

Jesus is my Saviour

I must believe that Jesus is God and that he can save me ******
Acts 16:31

Jesus

and I must submit to Jesus as King of my life.
Philippians 2:10-11

Christ Jesus came into the world to save sinners.

1 Timothy 1:15

Syllabus for On The Way for 3-9s

	Year 1	Year 2	Year 3
	Book 1 (13 weeks)	**Book 6 (10 weeks)**	**Book 11 (13 weeks)**
Old/New Testament	In the Beginning (3) Abraham (6) Jacob (4) ✓	Samson (2) Ruth (2) Samuel (2) Saul (4) ✓	Jesus Meets (3) God's Rules (10)
	Book 2 (12 weeks)	**Book 7 (13 weeks)**	**Book 12 (14 weeks)**
Christmas *New Testament*	Christmas gifts (5) Jesus' Authority (7) ✓	The Christmas Story (4) Preparation for Service (4) The Promised Messiah (5)	Heavenly Messengers (5) Jesus Helps (5) Parables of the Kingdom (4)
	Book 3 (13 weeks)	**Book 8 (9 weeks)**	**Book 13 (13 weeks)**
New Testament *Easter* *Early Church*	Prayer (4) Jesus is King (5) Peter (4) ✓	Jesus Teaches (5) Parables of Judgment (2) The Easter Story (2)	Parables of the Vineyard (3) Jesus our Redeemer (3) The Early Church (3) Paul (4)
	Book 4 (10 weeks)	**Book 9 (10 weeks)**	**Book 14 (14 weeks)**
Old Testament	Joseph (4) Job (1) Moses (5)	David (7) Solomon (3) ✓	Kings (5) Daniel (4) Esther (2) Nehemiah (3)
	Book 5 (10 weeks)	**Book 10 (11 weeks)**	
Old Testament	In the Wilderness (4) Joshua (4) Gideon (2) ✓	Elijah (5) Elisha (4) Jonah (2)	

The books can be used in any order; the above plan is the suggested order.
The syllabus is chronological; Christmas to Easter is all about Jesus, followed by 3 series on the early church (1 in Book 3 and 2 in Book 13). The rest of each year consists of lessons from the Old Testament. Old Testament and New Testament lessons are in separate books (apart from Book 11), so the books can be used in whatever order is required. The books contain differing numbers of lessons, so that they fit the required number of weeks between Christmas and Easter and the following Christmas.
The number in brackets indicates the number of lessons in a series.

For more information about *On The Way for 3-9s* please contact:
Christian Focus Publications, Geanies House, Fearn, Tain, Ross shire, IV20 1TW / Tel: (01862) 871 011 or
TnT Ministries, 29 Buxton Gardens, Acton, London, W3 9LE / Tel: +44(0) 20 8992 0450

Teacher's Challenge Solution

pages
15, 87